Principles of Sufism

Nahid Angha, Ph.D.

ASIAN HUMANITIES PRESS
Fremont, California

ASIAN HUMANITIES PRESS

Asian Humanities Press offers to the specialist and the general reader alike the best in new translations of major works and significant original contributions to enhance our understanding of Asian literature, religions, cultures and thought.

Library of Congress Cataloging-in-Publication Data

Angha, Nahid.
    Principles of Sufism / Nahid Angha.
        p.   cm.
    Previously published: San Rafael, Calif. : International Association of Sufism Publications, 1991.
    Includes bibliographical references.
    ISBN 0-87573-061-2
    1. Maktab Tarighe Oveyssi Shahmaghsoudi. 2. Sufism. I. Title.
BP189.7.M28A55 1994
297'.4--dc20   94-29491
                                                                CIP

Printed in the United States of America

The learned are the heirs to the
knowledge of the prophets.

Prophet Mohammad

To Ali Kianfar, Shah Nazar
a learned and wise Sufi Master.

Acknowledgments

Special thanks to:

Roger W. Olmsted for his insightful editing.

Jeffery McCullough for his effort to track down many difficult-to-find reference materials and books.

Priscilla Hedges for the time and dedication she put into proofreading the manuscript.

Joe Pace for his assistance in preparing the manuscript for print.

Table of Contents

In the Name of Allah
Most Gracious, Most Merciful,
the Essence of the Eternal Book,
the Beginning and the End,
the Apparent, and the Hidden.

Introduction

It is for us to open the gateway of knowledge to the human
being, and so make knowledge the light of the way
and understanding the light of the aware heart.
Moulana Shah Maghsoud

The pursuit of truth is the quest for a particular goal, a
quest pursued no matter how difficult the path—and for the
most important truths, the way may be long and arduous indeed. *Tasawouf,* or Sufism, is the esoteric school of Islam,
founded on the pursuit of spiritual truth as a definite goal to
attain: the truth of understanding reality as it truly is, as
knowledge, and so achieving *ma'arefat.* In *Tasawouf* when
we speak of understanding or cognition we refer to that perfect self-understanding that leads to the understanding of the
Divine. This very logical principle is based on a typically succinct saying of Prophet Mohammad: "Whoever knows oneself, knows one's Lord."

The origins of *Tasawouf* can be traced to the heart of
Islam in the time of the Prophet, whose teachings attracted a
group of scholars who came to be called "ahle suffe", the
People of Suffe, from their practice of sitting at the platform of
the mosque of the Prophet in Medina. There they engaged in
discussions concerning the reality of Being, and in search of
the inner path they devoted themselves to spiritual purification and meditation.

The ahle suffe believed that it was the unique human
right and privilege to be able to find the way towards understanding the reality of the Divine. As the cognitive tools of
ordinary mental logic are limited in their ability to comprehend such a great and all-embracing subject, disputation and

all discussions based on language alone cannot open any door to understanding such reality. Instead, such a path of understanding necessitates spiritual striving, the understanding and the knowledge of the heart, in its quest to realize the existence of the Divine. Such an approach separates Sufis from philosophers, and indeed from any other group of scholars whose knowledge is founded upon traditions, words, assumptions, and the imagination instead of the actual and direct understanding of all that exists. Thus the path of Sufis, of cognizant Moslems, was separate from that of traditional understanding. They became the people of the *tarigh*, or the way; their particular goal was to understand and introduce the esoteric aspect of Islam, as opposed to the exoteric public elements of this universal religion.

The principles of Sufism are all based upon the rules and teachings of the Koran and the instructions of the Prophet. To a Sufi there is no gulf of separation between all of Being, the Creator, and His creations. That the multitude cannot perceive this fundamental unity is the result of the impurity of *nafs* and the limitations of the material and physical tools that mankind possesses. If man were free from the limitations of matter, then he would surely witness this immense and eternal unity of Being. But there is a chance for mankind to ascend to such a level of understanding, a pathway that can be followed through purification and meditation to the realization of its achievement. When one's heart is purified, the manifestation of the Divine is reflected in the mirror of the heart. Only then may man ascend from the level of his animal nature to the level of the true human being.

Since all the principles that underlie the instructions of Sufis are based on the Koran, it is impossible to relate Sufism to any religion outside of Islam. Yet the search for true understanding and abstract knowledge of reality is a universal quest. As long as humanity endures, so too will the search for such understanding continue. History shows us that every nation and religion has its own way of expressing the universal spiritual quest.

The Origin of the School of Sufism

In order to understand Sufism and its origin we must briefly touch on the elements of studies that have been undertaken in the hope of understanding Sufism, and so examine the accuracy of the conclusions that scholars have drawn. To do so, the reader should keep in mind a few important caveats while studying the information that has been collected concerning Sufism. Sometimes the lack of truly thorough research, or the difficulties inherent in translating from one language to another, have led to confusion instead of enlightenment. As a result, Sufism is often only half understood, with that understanding further clouded by interpretations and the biases of commentators. These limitations have made tracing the road to Sufism's origin difficult, even for accomplished scholars. Even should the scholar choose his sources very carefully, the barrier of language yet remains, an important factor hindering the passage of truth.

There have been many debates concerning the origin of Sufism and how this school of inner knowledge was established. In seeking the spiritual and intellectual ancestry of Sufism, some have looked toward Greek philosophy in general and Platonism especially, some to the Hermetic Christianity of the gnostics of the late Roman Empire, and others to Buddhism or Yogism. But Sufism, as it has been practiced since its birth, is quite a different school of belief, practice, and goal than any of these pre-existing ways of thinking. Even though Sufism, as the school of spiritual knowledge based on self cognition as the door toward understanding the realities of Being, is a school open to all humanity, it was born out of Islam and is the heir to the treasures of knowledge from the sacred heart of the Prophet Mohammad, and has practiced its way accordingly. The actual birth of Sufism as a way of thought and practice is therefore subsequent to the advent of Islam.

The history of the origin of Sufism records that during the lifetime of the Prophet Mohammad, fifteen centuries ago, there was a group of pious individuals from different nations who, guided by the Laws of Islam, sought for the direct experience of the Divine. Companions of the Prophet, they were people of principles practicing certain disciplines and meditations for the sake of purification, the realization of Divine love, and the understanding of reality. They were the Lovers of God who sought union with Him through losing the limited self in His Divinity (*fana*), and remaining alive in that Reality (*bagha*).

These individuals met on the platform, or suffe, of the mosque where Prophet Mohammad used to pray in Medina, Arabia. They would meet there almost every day to discuss the ways to inner knowledge, the truths of revelation, and the meanings of the verses of the Koran. Thus the platform of that mosque in Medina became the first gathering place of one of the most influential groups in the history of mankind's spiritual civilization. They were called ahle suffe, the People of the Platform.

These individuals cultivated the seed of a school of spiritual practice based on knowledge of the self, and thus free of the trappings of tradition and superstition, a knowledge of the inner heart apart from the customary beliefs of their contemporary society as well as those of future civilizations. It is from this group that all the schools of Sufism that have ever existed owe their origin, for by pursuing the path of unsullied inner knowledge they were the founders of Sufism, and the binding link between its subsequent developments.

Among the most famous were: Salman Farsi, Ammar Yasser, Balla'al, and Abdullah Masoud; some historians have added Oveyse Gharani to this list as well. Avoiding proselytizing among the multitude, their gatherings were held in private, open only to true seekers of reality. Instead of preaching in public, these pious individuals were searchers of truth, not performers of rhetoric.

After the Prophet passed away, each of the people of suffe returned to his homeland to instruct students eager to follow upon the path of inner knowledge. There they became the great missionaries of Islam. History shows that within a century or two their style of self-understanding and discipline were introduced by their students to nations as diverse and widely separated as Persia, India, Indonesia, Syria, Egypt, Mesopotamia, and North Africa. Their teachings were based on individual understanding and direct experience, not just on particular texts or rote learning. In this manner, their fundamental teachings have been preserved in their style up to the present, instead of withering away into the empty formulas of scholasticism.

Through this process of diffusion, different schools and orders of Sufism gradually emerged from the single original group of suffe at Medina. Their practices differ from one another in emphasis and doctrine, but all legitimate Sufi schools trace their ultimate origins back to the original group of the Prophet's spiritual disciples.

The Origin of the Word *Tasawouf*, ' Sufism'

A majority of scholars believe that the word "*Tasawouf*" derives from the word "suf", which means wool. This assumption is based on a story told regarding the reason for wearing woolen garments by the pious people of the first century of Islam. It has been narrated that the Prophet and faithful Moslems wore garments of wool to denote their detachment from the world and simplicity in living. Within a century after the emergence of Islam, Arabs, who were mainly desert peoples, had conquered great empires such as Persia and Egypt. These conquering Arabs surrounded themselves with a luxury hitherto unknown to them in their spartan desert lives. The more pious individuals of the Moslem community feared that the message of Islam was in danger of being completely lost through the decadent example of these Arab conquerors who professed to spread the Prophet's words. Looking back to the severe simplicity of Islam's beginnings, and remembering those early pious Moslems of Medina, they decided to clothe themselves in rough wool as a gesture of protest against the profligacies of their leaders. Guarding themselves against the temptations of luxury, they set themselves apart from the lower material life. These pious ones performed fasting, mortification, and denied themselves the pleasures of material life to the greatest extent possible.[1] Wearing wool thus became a part of the discipline connected to Sufism. But even though Sufis wore suf, wool, from the very beginning of Islam, the word "Sufism", according to Arab grammar, is not a derivative of the word suf, and not whoever wears suf is a Sufi.[2] Or as Sheikh Saadi, a great Persian poet and sage said:

> The goal of the people of the inner path is not their outer garments.
> Serve the King yet remain a Sufi.

Other scholars believe that the word "Sufi" derives from the word "sufateh", the name of a thin plant. Sufis were usually thin because of extreme mortification and fasting. Thus they were likened to sufateh as a symbol for their emaciation.[3] But, as in the preceding theory, this assumption is not linguistically or grammatically correct.

Another group of scholars claim that the word "Sufism" is a derivative from the Greek word "Soph", meaning wisdom or knowledge.[4] But this assumption does not seem right either. Aside from the different spellings, Sufis, and especially the Sufis of the first few centuries, denied that philosophy could be a fitting tool for understanding reality, since through its reliance on verbal descriptions and limited reasoning philosophy would actually obscure rather than reveal the truth of reality. For example, Rumi says:

> Those who only reason have wooden legs
> And wooden legs give an unsteady gait.

Or Sanai, another great Sufi (12th century) says:

Do not call philosophy
religion
And do not call the ignorant
wise.

Even though Sufis were learned individuals, still we cannot equate "Sufism" with "philosophy" and "Sufi" with "phi-
losopher", for their foundations of knowledge and practices
were very different. And as well, linguistics reveals that this
attempted derivation is mistaken.[5] Unfortunately, this mistake
has perpetuated itself throughout much of the research regarding the origin of the word "Sufism", recurring over and
over again. The reason lies in the unfamiliarity of the researchers not only with the beliefs and mentality of the Sufis,
but also with the nuances of the Arabic language.

There is also yet another idea regarding the word
Sufism. It seems that before the time of the Prophet
Mohammad there was a group of very pious people who
worked as the servants of the Kaaba. These people were
called "Sufe".[6] Their practices included mortification and the
avoidance of any physical pleasures. Some assume that the
word "Sufism" is a derivative form the word "Sufe", but this
assumption does not bear close examination, as the rules of
Arabic grammar as well as the different styles of the practice
make its fallacy evident. Some Sufis have practiced mortification, but this discipline has not been a general rule in Sufism,
while others disapprove of any kind of mortification. Etymo-
logically, "Sufi" is not a derivative of the word Sufe; histori-
cally Sufis were a group of Moslem intellectuals forming a
School of an inner path based on the instructions of the
Prophet Mohammad and the teachings of the Koran. Necessarily, this school had to be established after the advent of
Islam and not before.

Even though many efforts have been made to discover
the origin of the word, they do not give us a clear understanding about the word *Tasawouf.* It would seem that under-

standing the origin of Sufism, either the school or the word it denotes, is as mysterious as the whole practice of the Sufis. There are also other explanations about Sufism which are all literary descriptions based on the practices of the Sufis. I will mention some as follows: Sufism is piety and the purifying of the heart; it is avoiding bad temper and base qualities; it is remembering God; it is an essence without form; it is annihilation in the Almighty; it is secret; it is inner purity; it is closeness to reality; it is eternal life. The Sufi is a person of principles; or he is absent from himself and present with God. Each one of these descriptions refers to a discipline and practice performed by Sufis; none embraces all the essence of Sufism.

Our examination of the various attempts to account for the origin of the word Sufism shows the limitations of traditional scholarly inquiry when it attempts to approach the Divine. This reflects the greater difficulty of academic research in attempting to explain a way of understanding that transcends the limits of human knowledge. It would seem that despite the efforts of many scholars, we come to the understanding that actually no one knows the origin of the word *Tasawouf*—and, it might be added, the full reality of Sufism as well. Just as Sufism cannot be explained in terms of earlier gnostic schools, so it appears that Sufism is not a word derived from a pre-existing root word; the school of Sufism is not an explanation of a practice. And its believers are those who have mastered profound and mysterious principles introduced by Islam, principles never classified before.

The attempt of this brief work is to outline some of the doctrines that are essential to Sufism and most especially those principles which, when practiced and perfected, can make an individual cognizant in the realm of inner travelling. Sufism is best understood when we learn about it through the explanation of one of the most influential figures among Sufis. He reveals the mystery of the word Sufism (*Tasawouf*) as well as introducing those principles which make a seeker a

Sufi. This teacher, Imam Ali, was the cousin and the son-in-law of the Prophet Mohammad.

Historians have recorded that he was the only child born in the House of God, Kaaba. In the same house, he died with equal grace and dignity. Amir-al-Moumenin Ali was the first man who believed in Islam. He was the heir of the heritage of the prophecy whose guidance throughout the fifteen centuries of the life of Sufism has been the greatest inspiration for many . It has been narrated from the Prophet who said,"I am the City of Knowledge and Ali is the Gate." To Moslems, he is the King of the believers; to the Sufis he is called *Valli*, the Guide. He is the Light of the way, without which the realization of reality would be an impossible task.

Sufism is best described by the words of this mysterious teacher. It is narrated from Amir-al-Moumenin Ali (as well as Imam Sadegh, his grand son) who said that *Tasawouf* is an acronym of four letters. (*Tasawouf* is a four letter word: TSVF and pronounced *Tasawouf* in its original language.) Each letter holds a secret representing one stage or quality of a Sufi. Together the word TSVF makes the twelve Principles;[7] one who perfects these principles is a Sufi.

T, the first letter stands for three practices of: *Tark* (abandonment); *Tubeh* (repentance); and *Tugha* (virtue).

S, the second letter of the word stands for another three qualities to be perfected by a *salek*: *Sabr* (patience); *Sedgh* (truthfulness and honesty); and *Safa* (purity).

V, the third letter stands for: *Vud* (love); *Verd* (*Zekr* and remembrance); and *Vafa'a* (faithfulness).

F, the final letter, represents another three qualifications: *Fard* (solitude); *Faghr* (poverty); and *Fana* (annihilation).

During a life of learning, practicing, and teaching Sufism under the guidance and instruction of one of the greatest Sufi Masters of all time, Moulana Shah Maghsoud, my physical and spiritual father, I came to the realization that the door toward knowledge may open to afford a glimpse or two of reality to a seeker, but without mastering these twelve principles, such understanding will not remain clear for long. After passing through many *chelleh*,[8] I discovered that each stage of these disciplines opens up a new door to the eternal graceful knowledge, and so reveals a new secret. It is only through perfecting these stages that the seeker can break the boundary of the limited self and remain not a solitary drop from the ocean of life, but become one with the ocean itself and experience the meaning of the magnificent Message of *la illaha illa Allah*: that there is no limited self, everything is the Existence, the Eternal, God, Allah. It is then that Existence after complete annihilation of the Sufi remains eternally as it truly is, without cover, without secret.

When the curtain of illusion fell there was only One, no one but God.

Many times I have been asked what exactly each practice means and what are the appropriate manners, disciplines, and qualities that a *salek* must have in order to attain mastery and so become a part of this spiritual path. Therefore, in each chapter I have explained the meaning of each practice and related disciplines and manners. Many times I have referred to the wisdom of the ancient Sufis, since without the guidance of the teachers no path can be successfully traversed. Each principle directs the individual towards the path of recognition of the essence within, the essence hidden behind the veils of change and the curtains of uncertainty. The aim of any intelligent human being should be found in the foundation of the truth of stable tranquility and undisturbed survival, the goal of the final quest. To achieve such a goal one must free oneself from the imprisonment of the boundary of change and find a way to return to one's essential being and find the source of the infinite knowledge within.

It is only that pure essence of the self that is made manifest in the book of Being, where each word reveals a secret and every letter is engraved upon the face of Being, illuminating the image of the perfect human. As movements do not represent life, likewise change is not the being of existence, and whosoever stands on his feet is not necessarily the "Perfect Human", the Perfect Human who stands upon the heights of Sufism.

I have attempted to explain each Principle as completely as the limitation of words and space permits; the rest depends upon you who have to search within yourself.

> You are the subject of the Divine Book,
> ask for yourself.
> It is you, whom you are looking for.

Nahid Angha
February 4th, 1991

CHAPTER ONE

Tark (Abandonment)

Understanding frees you from the bondage
of attachments and
guides your steps with certainty toward the reality of
your truth.
Moulana Shah Maghsoud

Tark is the first principle for the *salek* to accomplish, having chosen the path of spirituality, since one's intentions are as important as the actions upon which their truth depends. The principle of *tark* is the abandonment of the world of illusion, and with it one's collection of transient beliefs that are based upon it. This involves the inner recognition that the superficial knowledge gathered through the experiences of life and the perceptions of senses is based on illusion instead of reality, and represents bondage instead of freedom. On the path of spirituality one must first learn to draw the fundamental distinction between deception and truthfulness. It is easy to fall into falsehood by thinking that one may appropriate the knowledge of others as one's own. Such mere information should not be mistaken for actual knowledge—although to do so is the norm of everyday life. We should all be aware of how misleading the perceptions of our senses can be, and even more so, the judgments that we draw from them. What we learn through our senses is limited information concerning the surface of Being that we will judge according to our past and present store of superficial knowledge. This limited information can hardly become the foundation from which to raise one's self to the level of understanding the knowledge of the abstract in its inward truthfulness. If a human being does not awaken from this dangerous illusion, he will undoubtedly remain entrapped in that deception until he shall die, never allowing himself the chance of tearing asunder the covers of illusion to find the truth that lies hidden behind. Man is the microcosm of the whole of existence; he has within himself the potential to understand the macrocosm, but only if he puts aside the illusions that make up the attachments to the world of limitations.

A student of Sufism avoids falling into falsehood by learning how not to mistake imagination and assumption for the truth of reality. Pursuing what is not ultimately real takes the seeker deeper into the gulf of unknown desires and longing for the material world. In order to reach the truth of ultimate reality which is the goal of a Sufi, one must remain in a stable balance, since living in harmony in the state of equilibrium is the environment that spirituality will have the chance to grow. The logic of this necessity is straightforward: When one is continuously pulled by the diverse cords of desires and transient information one cannot remain stable and in the state of equilibrium. Cutting the strings of attachments does not prevent one from enjoying life and learning how to approach the reality within, but rather disciplines one in the control of one's life. Instead of a limitation, it frees one from being controlled by all the unknown or even known forces that surround every one of us.

Teachers have instructed their students to practice three kinds of *tark*:

1. *tark* of the world of matter, which is to step beyond the world of illusion by understanding the limitations and the superficiality of the sense perceptions, as well as learning not to mistake mere information for knowledge,

2. *tark* of paradise, which is to leave the promises of an unknown tomorrow and remain steadfast in learning for the sake of understanding, instead of becoming greedy for a reward,

3. *tark* of *tark*, which consists in becoming free from the boundaries of dimensions and limitations. At this level the *salek* has freed himself from any attachments, including those of *tark*.

Before a *salek* receives any spiritual instruction from a Master, he must physically and mentally purify himself. Learning to be physically clean at all times teaches the student to help himself in correcting any bad or unpraiseworthy qualities or characteristics that he may possess. It also helps him to keep his environment clean, for impurity must be transformed into purity on the path of the spiritual journey if one is to ascend to the level of the perfect human.

Among the first cleansing that the individual must practice is the erasing and washing away of immorality and evil qualities he sees in himself. Wickedness and base manners are obstacles between the seeker and Divine glorification. The person seeking spirituality seeks a tranquility that impurities prevent. The same rule exists for a man's environment, habitation, and worship. One parallel to this is the modern subject of ecology; the pure balance which ecology demands has been a practice ever kept sacred by Sufis and their students. Impurity holds no promise. It cuts the continuation of life short. A human being should not only establish his own survival in the most promising manner but also for the betterment and the survival of his environment, generation, culture and the world in general. Whatever prevents a human being from such accomplishment is in fact impurity. Badness reflects the inner state of constant struggle and emotional turmoil. Unless one frees oneself from these agents of self-destruction, one will not arrive at the gateway of life.

Sufi masters have also instructed their students in the practice of taming and controlling the temptations of their *nafs*. The term "*nafs*" has more than one meaning in Sufism. *Nafs* have sometimes been related to the western conception of the character or personality, and at other times to the different qualities of human nature which, like veils, cover and conceal the true identity of the self .

In general, *nafs* have been divided into the following six categories:

nafs of *lavameh* which include deception, anger and egotism;

nafs of *mulhameh* which consist of generosity and patience;

nafs of *mutmaeneh* including worship and contentment;

nafs of *amaareh* encompassing greed, jealousy, passion, and arrogance;

nafs of *razieh*, which are purity and meditation; and *marzieh,* which includes thinking.[1]

Learning how to tame *nafs* refers to avoiding those inferior qualities of *nafs* that can overcome the heart and mind of the seeker and prevent him from progressing on the spiritual path. Human being follows his mind and his heart at all times. His learning, his experiences, his emotional states, his aspiration, goals, and morals all contribute to his style of living and his contribution to himself as well as his surrounding. If the mind and the heart of a person are glorified by praiseworthy and superior qualities, filled with high aspiration and dedication, and are grounds for learning and knowledge, then the person of such mind and heart can ascend to the level of spirituality and step beyond the world of limitations, as he is attracted to a higher stage of being. However, if an individual overlooks such necessity, then he is an enemy to himself as well as his surroundings, since he is a man of no knowledge and the person of no knowledge cannot distinguish between goodness and wickedness, purity and impurity, survival and destruction. The person with inferior qualities is a person who is attracted to the lower stage of being. The desires of the *nafs* extinguish the light of divine love in the heart of the *salek*. A person who is searching for a spiritual path to ascend his being to a higher level has to cultivate higher qualities in his heart and mind and remain stable and strong at all times so not to become motivated by the lower qualities of *nafs* such as jealousy, greed, and egotism. The lower and worthless qualities of *nafs* will disturb the tranquility within, they become the chains fasten the human mind to the short lived waves of life and distract him from the essence of his being.

To transform them into praiseworthy qualities will add to the peace and tranquility of the mind, thus leading the way to a truthful understanding of one's being.

Some spiritual seekers have said that the nature of the lower *nafs* is built upon impoliteness, for the lower *nafs* unceasingly assail the purer faces of the living, may fall into hypocrisy to reach a goal, and may practice deception to achieve a status. Such qualities imprison the self and conceal the truth of reality from the seeker. It has been said that whoever is led by n*afs* also accompanies *nafs,* and whoever serves *nafs* receives corruption from *nafs* as his reward.[2]

One must note that any quality that deprives one of balance and stability may also become a potential source of inner corruption. Thus, not only low qualities are sources of impurities; even an ordinarily praiseworthy quality that is colored by selfishness and egotism which ultimately deprives a person of his balance and stability will become the source of corruption. But one does not need to remain possessed by low qualities, or be a slave to *nafs.* It is possible for an individual of essential wholesomeness to purge himself of the impure and begin the path of ascension. Such a transformation is not a matter of happenstance; it has its own inner logic that can be understood as a basis for practice.

The list of the superior and inferior qualities within any human being is a long one, as the being of humanity is a being with a long list of desires, a system of many diverse qualities, a book of constant changing moralities. The proper being of man is the abstract essence within the changing nature, a limitation longing for infinity, a being who demands eternal survival. As there are human beings, there are descriptions to them that are all unique in nature. Thus, we have no choice but to mention a few.

Among the inferior qualities of *nafs* are selfishness, greed, and jealousy. It has been narrated from the Prophet that, "There are three qualities that accompany all wickedness, avoid these three with all your power. Avoid selfishness since selfishness caused the Devil not to bow to Adam. Avoid greed since greed caused Adam to taste the forbidden fruit; and avoid jealousy as it caused the sons of Adam to kill each other."³

What we call human is a being who possesses an intellect as well as the spirit of sensuality. The sensual spirit urges him to yield to the lower desires that are the necessary and elemental qualities which sustain the generation of the physical world. But the human being also has the intellect that allows him to enrich his life with those higher qualities that enable him to understand the existence of himself. If the animal *nafs* overcomes the intellect, indecent morals will surface like dead fish in a lake, and the individual will be torn by struggles and restlessness within. Base morals may be likened to fire and war which do not afford the individual a respite or offer a chance for peace.⁴

Selfishness is a lower quality of *nafs* that Sufis instruct their students to strongly avoid. The selfish individual sees himself as higher than all others, always right while others are invariably wrong, but this deception in fact prevents him from learning and advancing his true self. The selfish person is, in fact, typically lowly, of base origins, though the vice of selfishness may infect any. Such a person will, in his moral solipsism, naturally disrespect the rights of others. The arrogant forget all the rules of politeness, becoming like the Devil who saw himself as higher than Adam.⁵ The Devil said, "I am better than he. Thou created me of fire, whilst him Thou didst create of mud." (Koran: XXXVIII,76) The nature of selfishness is, then, like the fire continuously burning the selfish through distraction and ignorance.⁶

A mind which has been overcome by selfishness cannot settle into righteousness, because of the ignorance inherent in arrogance. As Amir-al-Moumenin Ali (seventh century) has said, selfishness is the center of arrogance. A selfish man becomes so proud of his inconsequential knowledge that he convinces himself that his bit of information is a profound understanding. Therefore, through his own arrogance he will prevent himself from learning. He sees others as lower than himself, incapable of teaching him anything. There is ignorance within the selfish, yet he sees ignorance within others. Egotism is born from such arrogance, and arrogance in turn springs from empty desires. The egotist walks on the earth so proud of himself that the very grains of sand despise him.[7]

Such great misunderstanding of a selfish and arrogant person can also be found in the mentality of those who have but a fistful of information and think of it as a great discovery. They may as well see the roads that others take to approach reality as incorrect. For example, a scientist who is drowned in his thinking process and does not look into the truth of the spiritual teachings of great masters is keeping himself from attaining a greater knowledge. He is no better than a religious fanatic who is threatened by the advancement of science. They both are arrogant and arrogant is deprived from true knowledge as his mind is narrow, his personality is imprisoned by illusions created by himself, and he worships an unknown god. In truth, he is an idol worshipper and an idol is nothing but the creature of illusion created for the sake of fear or greed.

The Prophet has said that faith and arrogance do not mix...; the commitment to selfishness and arrogance is even worse than any sin.... [8] The reason for this primacy of selfishness is because it prevents one from truthful understanding. If someone understands his mistakes and learns about his shortcomings and limitations, he will correct them, but arrogance sees inner correctness at all times. How can he even allow himself the chance for melioration?

One small particle of selfishness cannot enter paradise, just as one small particle of faith does not enter hell.[9]

Linked to selfishness, and yet distinct from it, is another inferior quality of the lower *nafs*, namely jealousy. One who is jealous resents and feels at odds with others. He despises people as if they were barriers preventing him from living as he would wish. The fire of jealousy so destroys the person by keeping peace of mind away from him. A jealous person is miserable, busying himself with the thoughts of others, instead of dwelling in his own house, he is constantly distracted by the dwellings of others. Such distraction becomes his second nature, and the jealous person will live and die with this quality, never giving himself the chance of freedom. And so he will lose his harmony and equilibrium now and forever.

Sufis believe that jealousy and infidelity are close partners. If jealousy leaves the heart, the tongue frees itself from gossip and the mind from accusations. When an individual learns to avoid immorality, he will find no time to busy his mind with the thoughts of others, especially if those thoughts are nourished by jealousy. One who feeds his heart with the poison of jealousy is deprived of the Mercy of God.[10] Like a tyrant, jealousy is born of cruelty and injustice, and it will not depart and allow peace.[11]

Another low quality to be avoided is hypocrisy, for the hypocrite is a liar who acts to please others. Such a person has no truthfulness in his actions and cannot therefore be worthy of trust. The best and most common example of the hypocrite is the ignorant person who pretends to have knowledge, and so grasps the ideas of others while believing them to be his own. Proud of the borrowed information he has gathered, he forgets the immense true knowledge within. The hypocrite and his deeds lie in disgrace, for his intention does not agree with his action; he is a person who lives on dishonesty and disrespect, dwelling far away from the possibility of peace and harmony with himself, others, and his surroundings.

Anger is another habit that must be tamed in order to work for the good. When anger overcomes a human being, he will become like a savage animal. His desire to fight and attack others will bring danger to those around him, and so he becomes a source of corruption. Anger is also considered as a source of disturbance, emotional and physical distress. A *salek* seeks peace and balance; anger throws him off balance. An individual who seeks inner guidance needs to guard his mind and his heart from all the unwanted waves and impurities. Anger is like a fire; ugly deeds are its flames.[12]

Many Sufis, such as Hazrat Mir Ghotbeddin Mohammad, the author of *Destination: Eternity* and Ghotbeddin Abdul Mozafar, the author of *Sufi Nameh*, have written that the human being has two counselors: passion that acts as a sympathetic counsel, and anger that acts as a guardian and keeps all which is disliked away from the person. If the law falls into the hands of these two guardians, justice will be replaced by injustice, and corruption will overwhelm all. But if these two counsels work under the instructions of intellect, goodness wins and wickedness loses. On the other hand, if the power of passion, lust, and anger increase, the human being becomes corrupted and loses his generosity. A human being who is seeking spiritual guidance needs to avoid desires and qualities which lead him towards the road of corruption. Corruption is the destruction of purity which hides the reality within. Corrupted qualities occupy the mind and the heart of a human being and will not let the essence and identity manifest itself. They become the owners and the self becomes their slave.

Moulana Shah Maghsoud wrote that, "Heart is the House of God, why do you fill it with the desires of the *nafs*, ignorance and darkness? You will turn to these idols, worship them and ask for their help. You have employed the Eternal God to glorify your idols, until the hand of justice shall drag down your despising idols and punish them. That will be a time of great pain. Your masters and rulers will be disgraced and your share of their ruin will be loss and torture."[13] Idols are nothing but the imaginary masters that one holds so sacred within his heart and mind and worships them. Whether it be material wealth, fame, illusive ideas, unknown gods, or carved stones—all are idols created by those who do not know better. These idols are the creations of man, but at once also his master.

It is not enough to erase the bad and low qualities from one's being; the person who is seeking the path of spirituality must encourage himself to learn and practice praiseworthy qualities, those qualities that help him and his surroundings toward the road of tranquility and harmony, as it is tranquility which is the perfect ground for understanding, and it is harmony with the rules of the existence that opens the door towards truthful discovery.

One of the disciplines that one must master is the practice of politeness, both outer and inner. To keep the discipline of politeness, a *salek* must learn how to avoid his inappropriate manners and careless qualities. The worthless qualities and inappropriate manners are: indulgence, laziness, gluttony, and worthless emotionality. A *salek* practices strong discipline so as to overcome undesirable attractions, while controlling his body and mind. The intellectual identity of a human being should not become a slave to the petty currents of life. Self, body, heart, and mind must work in harmony hand in hand to accomplish the journey of a *salek* under the guidance of the aware intellect.

There are many practices taught by Sufis to overcome physical and mental laziness, such as decreasing the amount of food and sleep. Through such practice a *salek* learns to control his needs instead of being controlled by them.

Abu Abdullah Khafif Shirazi was one of the greatest Sufis of the ninth century. It is narrated that he used to fast every day, breaking his fast with seven raisins at sunset. And he would spend all night long meditating and praying.

Another story is told of Oveyse Gharan, who was believed to be one of the People of Suffe. He lived in Yemen during the time of the Prophet who many times had said, "I smell the fragrance of the Divine from the direction of Yemen", referring to the extent of Oveys' piety. Oveyse used to perform prayers and meditation for seven nights while standing. The next seven nights he would perform them while prostrating, and then the following week while sitting; during all these times he would continue to fast. It is narrated that once he felt sleepy and hungry after those twenty one days of fasting and meditation. He cried and called upon Allah, "Refuge, be to God, I am ashamed of these eyes wanting to sleep all the time, and this hungry stomach wanting to indulge itself in gluttony." And then he returned to his prayers. It is only the person of discipline who finds superiority in attaining self-knowledge over the indulgence of the body. Otherwise, reducing the amount of food or sleep without aiming toward self- knowledge is only a waste of time since it will not make a human being a sage.

Over all the practice of correcting one's shortcomings and changing lower qualities into superior ones makes a person a stronger human being, a being who will not be attracted by the demands of nature, rather he decides on his destination. While he lives in harmony and peace with nature, respecting and keeping it sacred, he makes himself stronger than the temptations of the world. A man who is stronger than the world's temptations is stronger than the world itself. Such a man will choose and demand rectitude from himself as well as from others. He and his like will become the leaders of true human civilizations.

The second *tark* is the *tark* of paradise, as a seeker should learn to find the ways toward self cognition and understanding the reality of the Divine. Paradise is a metaphor for reward while hell is for punishment. In traditional belief if a man commits himself to that which is forbidden, as instructed by custom and general belief, he or she will face punishment under human law while alive, or more likely under Divine law after he dies. If he acts according to the traditions, then he will be rewarded with paradise. These punishments and rewards are usually thought to occur after death. Such greed for reward and fear of punishment is expected from a person who worships the unknown. The individual who seeks understanding of the essence of his being should abandon the thoughts of paradise and hell, as these are promises of an unknowable tomorrow, the expectations led by worshipping the Divine out of imagination, illusion, or imitation—or ignorance. The goal of the Sufi is the truth of the Divine, not an imitation of it.

The intention of the *salek* is not concerned with any reward or punishment, as the way of the Sufi is to raise his being to a higher state. An increase in the knowledge of truth is the goal of the Sufi, not the achievement of dwelling in a heavenly place after his death. He learns that the position of man may be higher than both.

When a *salek* learns and perfects the controlling of the temptations of the world and the cleansing the of lower qualities from his being, then he is able to *tark* his *tark*. This third *tark* is usually a practice limited to the perfect human being who has stepped beyond any bondage and desires of *nafs*.

One of the most important counsels that Sufis give to their students is to purify their hearts; such purification replaces the shortcomings of nature with the light of knowledge. When impurities or the darkness of limitations are erased from the mirror of heart, the essence of self becomes more visible for the seeker to witness. It is only after purification that the seed of the spiritual child is cultivated in the human heart. Before complete cleansing of the impurities any cultivation is bound to miscarry. Unless purity rises from impurities, man will remain in the trap of darkness and ignorance forever. But once the heart is illuminated by the ray of divine knowledge, the child of eternity will step out of the world of change and enter the higher realm of truth. This second birth is reserved only for the pure.

Other praiseworthy qualities to master are humility, contentment, and meditation in solitude.

"Successful indeed are the believers, who are humble in their prayers." (Koran:XXIII,11) A humble person is not a person who submits himself to the will of others, but an individual who can piously extinguish the temptations and desires of *nafs* and light the rays of homage in his heart until desire perishes and heart lives.[14] Outward gestures do not represent meekness; the locus of humility is heart. A Sufi saw a man sitting, holding his knees and bowing his head. He said, "Oh, ignorant man, humility is in the heart not on the knees."[15] Meekness is a treasure which is not open to selfishness and dishonesty.

Sufis have talked about three kinds of humility: the humility of the beginner, that of the intermediate student, and that of the superior individuals. Practicing to master discipline and avoid temptations is the humility of the beginner. Receiving Divine manifestations and qualities in the heart, and annihilation into the Divine destiny is the humility of the intermediate ones. Receiving and preserving Divine essence in the spirit and annihilation of one's being into the infinite Being is the humility of those superior beings who have reached the highest possible realization.[16]

Sufis consider contentment to be a praiseworthy quality. Contentment consists in the absence of needs and desires, freedom from greed, and leaving whatever is in the hands of others. Contentment is a never-ending treasure. Sheikh Khafif Shirazi says that a person who is content does not ask to be given whichever is not in his hand, and he is not a slave to whatever he owns.[17]

Solitude has also been advised by the Masters. Solitude has two meanings: isolation from the bad habits of *nafs*, and isolation from the crowd. A seeker needs to practice isolation for the sake of better concentration, to attract spiritual waves and energy, and to preserve his strength in becoming attuned to the superior magnetic energies. Forty days of solitude has been advised in many religions. For example, Moses was ordered forty days of solitude. "And when We did appoint for Moses thirty nights of solitude and added to them ten, and he completed the whole time appointed by his Lord of forty nights..." (Koran:VII,142) Prophet Mohammad said, "For one who purifies one's self for forty days and nights the springs of wisdom will flow from one's heart into one's tongue." Purification of heart cleanses the heart of the distractions of everyday events and helps to concentrate on understanding the reality of the Divine. Sheikh Shahabeddin Suhrevardi , a Sufi Master, in clarifying the saying of the Prophet, writes in a beautiful story-like explanation that when the Almighty Lord wanted to give Adam a caliphate, he created him suitable for this world. He created Adam as a creation made of earthly elements. This creation took forty days and in each day a quality was added to Adam. Each quality had its own attraction. Yet each quality became a veil preventing him from seeing the grace of Eternity. Each veil became a cause for distance from the world of the hidden and each distance brought the world of matter closer.[18]

Purifying one's heart for forty days is then to tear the veils of limitations one after the other so the sun of truthful knowledge shines and man discovers his true essence. Humankind lives according to the rules of nature, but should he overlook the strength of the essential light of wisdom and intellect within? Sufis say that the illumination of heart should remain the goal of a human being, and such illumination is accessible yet hidden behind the veils of nature. Thus the wisdom behind the practices embracing forty days of sincerity along with solitude is that in each day a veil is to be dropped bringing greater closeness to the Divine.

After forty days, the forty veils will fall, the human grace and purity will transcend the voyage of distance and step into the realm of Divine closeness which is the origin of knowledge and the realm of goodness and grace. When such a human being witnesses Divinity, his ambition will ascend and become free from the attachments of the world. The springs of wisdom and knowledge will run from his heart onto his tongue. Such purification should be accomplished in solitude. The sign of solitude is the advent of knowledge, and the advent of knowledge is the result of witnessing Divinity. Disciplines which should accompany solitude are: less eating, less talking, remembrance, the freeing of the mind from disturbances, and meditation and concentration.[19] The result of forty days of solitude is reaching the beginning of the spiritual discovery (*kashf*).

Some Sufis believe that solitude has five rules: do not hear; do not see; do not say; do not think; and do not be.

Moulana Shah Maghsoud has instructed solitude hand in hand with sincere worship and searching to reach the Beloved. It is only then that the dawn of fortune rises from the horizon of heart, completes inner and outer purification, and erases the sense of duty out of worship and obedience.

Tark is thus a discipline that instructs the *salek* to sever himself from the chains of attachments. But *tark* does not mean mere mortification, nor does it result in a denial of life. It teaches the seeker to become stronger and to learn to control his needs. It is ultimately the stability of heart and strength of will that helps the seeker toward the road of self cognition. To become stable one has to discipline one's own self, to take truth for truth and leave mistake to illusion, and so to step freely, beyond the realm of change, need, and mortality.

CHAPTER TWO

Tubeb (Repentance)

*Common people repent from their sins, Sufis
repent from ignorance.*
Zunnun, the Egyptian Sufi

Repentance literally means "to turn away", and that is
the turning back from an inferior state towards a superior
state. According to the tenets of religion, repentance is the
regret one properly feels after committing a forbidden act. In
Sufism it refers to breaking forth from the barriers that hinder
the seeker from reaching the ultimate Being. The direction of
a Sufi is towards God, the eternal Being. The *salek* follows
the direct and straight path that begins with himself and ends
in the Divine. He or she is to turn away from whatever dis-
turbs and distracts his going forward towards Divine knowledge. And as the *salek* through the practice of *tark* has
learned to erase the darkness of illusion from his *nafs* and has
practiced the mastery of being truthful in his quest, his turning towards anything other than the Divine would constitute
a falsehood.

The condition for such turning away is awareness, that
is, the recognition of the veils and curtains that separate the
seeker from his goal, and the penetration of these veils to
attain the truth that lies hidden behind them. As the *salek*
becomes more aware he also becomes more capable of learning how to overcome the veils; thus the attraction in his heart
turns away from all that is not the essence of Divinity.

Repentance consists in seeing the actual shortcomings,
limitations in potentiality and faults of the self and con-
sciously and knowingly turning away from them to find the
direction towards *bagh* (truth). It begins with knowledge and
ends in the realization of belief.

Awareness, then, is the basic pillar of the spiritual quest, it helps the seeker to distinguish the shortcomings of his actions, and to recognize deceits and helplessness in thought, so that the heart regrets such weakness and darkness, and strives for understanding. The first step that the spiritual traveller takes is to confess his ignorance and his lack of knowledge. Without such realization he will not strive for advancement as he does not see within himself weaknesses that are to be transformed into strengths. It is after truthful recognition of his potentialities that a *salek* can strive for betterment. Thus, the *salek* must repent from all but truth with eagerness in his heart for the discovery within.

Repentance is only possible after the enlightenment of the heart and the awakening of the mind. That is when the heart and mind awaken from ignorance and see the rays of knowledge that lie within. It is after such illumination that the *salek* turns his face and ultimately his heart away from the ignorance of worldly attachments and towards the purification and enlightenment of his heart. Thus elements of weakness are removed, and the enlightenment is strengthened. The individual with a heart and mind that are glorified with pure and spiritual strength, whose goal is self-cognition, is the one who will arrive at the gateway of understanding and achieve the knowledge of the Divine. Pious deeds rise from the pious heart: "And, O, ye believers, turn ye all together towards God, that ye may attain Bliss." (Koran: XXIV, 31) "Wash you, make yourself clean, put away the evil of your doings from before mine eyes; learn to do well..." (Isaiah I:16,17)

To do well one must first recognize the veil that keeps away the ultimate reality. In turning away from weakness towards strength the individual must have the essential eagerness and inner potentiality for such a transformation, and then find his way to a truthful teacher who will guide him onto the path of cognition.

To a seeker, whatever keeps him from witnessing the truth of Being is considered to be forbidden. Ignorance, darkness of heart and mind, wicked and lower qualities, limitations, instability, and injustice are among the forbidden. One must recall that 'forbidden' refers to all that keeps one from his truthful search for self understanding and abstract knowledge. The 'Forbidden' are the curtains that hide the reality within, the agents of death that must be eradicated from one's character. For some, this is not a realistic possibility: not all are suited to the path of understanding. But all are called to avoid the forbidden: "Therefore say unto the house of Israel, thus saith the Lord God; Repent, and turn yourself from idols; and turn away your face from all admonitions." (Ezekiel 14:6)

Idols for a Sufi are those illusions erected by ignorance. The *salek* leaves them and returns towards God, the Eternal, all Powerful, all Knowing. Such repentance is travelling from the outer world into the inner self; stepping away from impurities towards purities; turning the face from ignorance towards knowledge; breaking the borders of limitations and traveling towards infinity; discovering unity in the depth of multiplicity. That is the truth of repentance for a Sufi.

Teachers have divided repentance into categories suit able for different levels of people and different stages of potentiality. Repentance has been divided into four categories: the turning away from blasphemy, which is the repentance of the infidel; the turning away from wicked deeds and prohibited actions, which is the repentance of the corrupt; the turning away from bad manners and temper, which is the repentance of the pious; the turning away from anything other than the Divine, which is the repentance of the prophets and masters.[1]

Sheikh Ahmad Ja'am, a great Sufi of the twelfth century, said that different people must repent of different qualities. The sinful must repent of sin; the obedient to God must repent of seeing himself as obedient; the reader of the Koran must repent of the illusions of form; the knowledgeable must repent of jealousy. The truthful must repent from egotism; the honest from selfishness.[2]

The easiest repentance is that from an apparent mistake. The corrupt must prevent his eyes, tongue, hands, and feet from corruption if he is to repent. But the repentance of the just is very different. A just person is one who does not ruin the moments of his life wandering about. Instead, he calls upon his heart as a witness to his actions and intentions. He watches his step at all times. He prevents his senses from experiencing that which is not proper or rightful for them to perceive. A *salek* must restrain his hands from taking what is not proper for him to take. He must break his bad and useless habits and leave the house of limitations to dwell instead in the house of the Divine.[3]

Some Sufis have also categorized repentance into: the repentance of the common people, which is the avoidance of wickedness and the turning towards goodness; the repentance of the negligent, which is the avoidance of the corruption of action and the turning towards morality; the repentance of the pious, which lies in avoiding desires for the world. Repentance for a Sufi is the shunning of weakness in his striving to achieve purity and honesty. The Monotheist repents of seeing other than truth, thus he turns away from multiplicity to unity, and from manifestations to the absolute truth. The repentance of a young person is the result of aspiration, generosity, enthusiasm, and hope. And for the old, repentance is the result of weakness, fear, and disturbances.[4]

In every culture we come across a belief that everyone has a divine minister in his heart. If the heart can listen to its inner voice it is just, and when the heart is just the whole body functions rightly. An unjust heart becomes the source of corruption. Turning away from the unjust is only possible when the heart can hear the voice of rectitude. The heart that is content by its ignorance and has become the temple of the unknown, is the unjust heart. Such a heart is deaf to the voice of wisdom and does not repent from falsehood and thus does not turn towards truth.

A seeker needs to separate himself from any weakness and temptation, including bad friends and corrupt companions. Bad friends destroy integrity, are barriers to goodness, and direct individuals towards false beliefs and illusions. Among the false friends are those of the world of attachments: we all know that these attachments are temporary and do not hold any inner promise. Releasing oneself from such bondage is to venture to dwell in freedom. Ali ibn Mosa was an ancient Sufi, of whom it is narrated that once he, who at that time was the minister of the king, was passing by riding in a glorious richly ornamented cart. Someone asked a woman whom he might be. The woman replied that he was a slave to luxury who had been severed from the mercy of God, and that its deprivation had made him sick in heart. When ibn Mosa heard what the woman had said of him he came to a truthful realization, resigned from the court and the ministry of the king; leaving all that he had he took refuge in the House of God.[5]

Veils that cover the reality within deprive the heart from receiving Divine illumination. Deprivation of the heart is considered a shortcoming in Sufism. Such deprivation darkens the heart, and a dark heart cannot foster cognition. The heart must be polished like a mirror if the light of knowledge is to shine upon it. If the heart finds a cure for its blindness and becomes able to see, the owner of such a heart will step out from the ranks of the common people and enter the level of the chosen ones. If the heart remains darkened, cruelty will conquer it, and the cruel heart is the house of the Devil: the weight of its ignorance prevents the opening of the heart to illumination.[6] Such a heart is bound to die, for it has only lived in the realm of matter and never realized its superiority over the realm of change.

Sufis have said that two conditions accompany knowledge and worship: a heart that is free from bondage to others; and an appetite that is free from the desires for the world. If a seeker wishes for something, he is not sincere; and if he strives for his desires or satisfies the appetite for the world, he is the slave of the material world. He who is a slave to his desires is not honored, and he who vanquishes his desires avoids the forbidden and impurities. Only such an individual avoids bad deeds, bad friends, bad places, bad thoughts, jealousy, greed, selfishness, hatred, and hypocrisy.[7] If the blessing of the Divine should fall upon a person, the realm of knowledge and awareness will become open to him.

Knowledge is that standard which distinguishes goodness from wickedness, light from dark. One who seeks superficial closeness to the Divine must cleanse his visage, and whoever seeks inner closeness must cleanse his inner self. Outward cleanliness is attained with water; inner cleanliness is achieved through repentance. It is said that many people step towards the path of belief; none but a few become repentant.

Repentance may be likened to that mystical elixir which gives life to the heart and turns iron into gold. It is the conscience of the path and the bridge to unity. Imam Sadegh, one of the greatest teachers, said that the truly knowledgeable repent of the disturbances of the mind, while saints repent of the disturbances of the heart, the pious repent of the desires of the *nafs*, chosen ones repent of seeing other than God, and the common people repent of sin.

The ultimate repentance is repenting of the "self". Moulana Shah Maghsoud said that as long as "you", the limited self, stands out and covers the reality, you will not discover *hagh* (truth). When the "you" disappears as a barrier, the curtain between "you" and "*hagh*" will fall; the truth of "you" will be dissolved in the truth of "*hagh*"; the contamination of "you" and the resulting dualism of self and truth will disappear from your body and heart.[8] You become a monotheist in its true meaning.

CHAPTER THREE

Tugha or Taghva
(Virtue and Abstinence)

The masters of this world are the generous,
and the masters of eternity are the virtuous.
Amir-al-Moumenin Ali (seventh century)

Allah the Almighty said, "The most honored of you is the most righteous in the sight of God". (Koran:XLXI,13)

Taghva literally means abstinence. In religion, abstinence means obedience to Divine instructions and the avoidance of that which He forbids. In everyday life, abstinence refers to conducting oneself with rectitude, while avoiding self-indulgence. Sufis have remarked that virtue contains within itself the sense of keeping faults at a distance and separating oneself from the lower *nafs*. Of course, religious piety may also be the result of fear of punishment or the fear of separation. If one fears divine punishment, one will likewise avoid forbidden acts and obey the Laws. But in contrast to this negative obedience, virtue is a key to eternity that saves one from the fires of restlessness and change.

Abstinence is a part of virtue in that it involves abandoning all of the lower entanglements, or *nafs*, that keep one away from the Divine; yet at the same time abstinence involves not being distracted by the loss of such things, awaiting neither reward nor praise. To grasp on to what keeps one away from the Divine is to embrace destruction; to keep such things at a distance brings tranquility and peace. Naturally, the wise shun destruction and search for tranquility. If one properly fears separation from "Truth", one separates oneself from all but "Truth".

It is not enough to abstain from some things that are forbidden while continuing to indulge in others. Instead, one must cut all the strings of attachments to the world, since as one is drawn towards them one steps farther away from his own reality. An individual who fears separation from the truth will not rest until he is united with the ultimate Being. 'Fear' here refers to the sense of eagerness and the potentiality of becoming united with the ultimate truth.

When a believer would acquire grace from a spiritual journey and attain the fulfillment of his being, he must first purify himself from the excesses of the world of illusion, and free his heart from the bondage of love of the world. Even though abstinence and repentance are different in meaning, at the same time there are many similarities between them. It is said that the changeable world is the house of destruction, the home of suffering, and the place of turmoil and ruin. Superficially, the life of the world may seem soft, yet its inner nature is ultimately harsh. Like a slow but deadly poison, it will ultimately kill all who drink of it. In such a house of suffering, the lighter a burden the individual bears, the more fortunate he shall be.[1] Even though the material world is the bridge toward understanding the reality that lies within, it is but a changeable bridge and a perishable destiny. One who is wise makes the best of the conditions in which he lives, but will not be overwhelmed and buried by those conditions. The reason that the world has been called the house of destruction in many spiritual schools lies in the fact that earthly life is unstable. Such life follows the rules of constant change and contingent conditions. Constant change signifies constant birth and death, the state of continuous sowing and reaping. A wise individual is not attracted to transient conditions since they are the signification of death. A *salek* must learn how to avoid the trap of attachments to earthly matters if he is to search for everlasting life beyond the possibility of death. This freedom is the master key of spiritual travelling, because it allows the *salek* to step out of the realm of birth, death, and constant change. This rejection of attachment to the material world does not imply any denial of rules of nature. The Sufi strives to understand the material world while at the same time freeing himself from the attachments to it.

One of the practices which has falsely been ascribed to Sufism is mortification, which is the denial of the value of living. Sufis do not teach mortification, because the practice of mortification does not result in the cutting of the chains of attachment to one's own mentality. Denying the joys of life does not bring spiritual strength, since denial is a mere negation. To practice denial does not imply control over one's wishes and desires: Sufis practice for the purpose of becoming stronger than the call of any desire. Becoming the owners and the controllers of themselves, they are not tempted by what they see and are so not compelled to avoid seeing it. But although the needs of the physical body must be satisfied, a human being is not born merely to lead an animal existence.

Sufis understand that although eating, for example, is part of surviving, it is not the destiny of life. If an individual's life revolves around physical satisfaction, he is but another animal. The difference between the level of a human being and the being of an animal consists in the possibility open to man of seeking higher inspiration, searching for a truthful goal, looking for the reason of life, understanding the rules of nature, and ultimately discovering the knowledge within.

Death is the final expectation for people who lead worldly, materialistic lives, even though they may mistakenly hope otherwise. The wise who know of reality, use their earthly life as a bridge to pass over, not as a state to dwell in. Sufism suggests the way to avoid living the life of an indulgent beggar, to live instead the life of a sage who cannot be deceived by transient change into mistaking a temporary abode for an everlasting dwelling.

A man or woman who becomes greedy for the love of the material world is living out an ephemeral destiny, for the heart of such a person will die, and one whose heart is dead cannot strive towards the path of Divinity.[2] We must note that living the life of limitation is a natural condition for mankind, and not a mistake, forbidden act, or fault; nor is mortification, as a way of surpassing the world of limitation, a practice instructed by Sufis. However, we should not expect to receive from the world of limitation what it cannot deliver. People often foolishly expect the outer world to give them eternal life, infinite peace, tranquility of heart, and inner wealth. The material world may offer such expectations, but it cannot deliver what it may falsely promise. The sooner one understands this simple logic, the better he shall live. The world and its attachments cannot guarantee eternal life, neither before nor after death. The world likewise cannot truthfully promise any knowledge beyond the borders of finitude. One who lives by the rules of the world of limitation, will gather from it nothing but the limited. And limitation is a boundary that prevents the spirit from pursuing the knowledge of abstractedness.

Sufis believe that the desires of the world lead to greed and jealousy, qualities which turn an individual's direction towards the forbidden. For Sufis, forbidden acts are veils over the heart that bring darkness and ignorance in their train. When the forbidden is indulged, darkness obscures the light of knowledge within the heart. But should the heart overcome darkness and ignorance, it will uncover the light and purity within.[3] In so doing, the *salek* will finally discover a constant and stable continuity hidden within those changeable perishable conditions, a discovery that shall ensure his ultimate survival. He will find the certitude of rules and laws, and so, setting himself free from the limited finite world, he shall in return find life. The truth is that, "Ye may not despair over matters that pass you by..." (Koran: LVII, 23).

The pious heart is free from desires and will endure the hardships of the world easily.[4] One who is virtuous is aware of his actions, and his awareness helps him to avoid acts which end in destruction, and to avoid pursuing actions that involve only finite goals. "The treasury of wickedness profits nothing, but righteousness delivers from death. The Lord may bid suffer the soul of the righteous to famine, but He casteth away the substance of the wicked." (Bible: Proverbs: Chapter 10: 2-3)

While it is true that many systems of spirituality claim to reject attachment to the world, and promise life eternal, Sufism differs in seeking for the means of transcendence within the living self. Sufis reject the point of view of religions that teach that eternity is found only after death. Rather, if one seeks everlasting life, one must taste it in this life, and not expect it to be offered as a gift in an unknown promised future after death.

Sufis do not deny the rules of nature or the actuality of death, but they refuse to be slaves to these rules or follow them blindly. The master of his own life, it has been said that a Sufi creates by his own will. Through proper discipline, a seeker learns to gain control over his life and so to recognize the veil of change which hides the purity and stability of eternal knowledge that dwells within his heart. He learns to pass over the bridge between death to life, from hell to heaven. Such a realization is impossible so long as truth remains hidden behind the curtain of instability. Instability cannot promise any awareness over destiny and finality by its very nature; only knowledge can. Pure knowledge may be understood only in and through its purity, when it has been unveiled; it may not be seen when the observer is blind to purity. "Whoever is blind in his path remains blind thereafter." (Koran: XVII, 72) Sufis do not remain blind to the rules of Being; indeed they are the discoverers and so also the survivors. Neither their destinies nor their lives are ended by the hand of death.

In our present age as in times past, material possessions form an attachment that occupies the will and blocks the sight. Worldly possessions cannot open a door towards understanding Being and realizing the Divine; to the contrary, it is said that it is harder for a rich man to pass through the gates of heaven than it is for a camel to pass through the eye of a needle. Moses left the luxury of the Pharaoh's palace and retired to the mountains. There he only owned a cane, a pair of shoes, and a coarse robe. But when he was directed to face his God, even those trifling belongings became the source of pain. He was then ordered to, "Throw aside thy rod...". (Koran: XXVII, 10.)

Ibrahim, the father of the prophets, broke all of the idols, and such idol breaking is the rule for finding reality. Be aware of the idols that you worship; they may be disguised under a variety of masks: tear them down if you would be among the seekers of reality. During ancient times, people worshiped statues, stones, and the forces of nature which the idols represented, because they had found these forces to be stronger than themselves. Today, human beings have stored different images of the same idols in the temple of their hearts and worship them with the same primitive ignorance. By worshipping the unknown they deprive themselves of the joys of freedom, preferring to remain entrapped within the bondage of ignorance. They would rather remain the followers of an unconscious imitation of superstition than become the knowers of their own identities and proper destiny. Jesus, purest among the pure, instructed his followers to leave behind all that they possessed from the world; Prophet Mohammad advised his followers to free their hearts from the desires of the world. On the true and straight path, stability and equilibrium, cognition, and freedom from illusion, are the keys to spiritual awareness.

Abu Yazid Bastami, one of the greatest Sufis of all time, said that "It took me three days to perfect my abstinence. The first day I abandoned the world and whatever belonged to it; on the second day I abandoned futurity and whatever belonged to that; on the third day I abandoned everything other than the Glorious Lord: and on the fourth day nothing remained but the Almighty Lord."[5] Wisdom grows in the heart of the abstinent and abstinence is one of the pillars of purity, and it is attained after *nafs* repent of ignorance. Abstinence is then a stepping out from the realm of doubt and hesitation, both that which is apparent and that which is hidden within the heart. Outward abstinence is reliance on God; and inner piety is achieved when nothing enters the heart of the Sufi but the Almighty Lord.[6]

Mere avoidance of the forbidden is not virtuousness, nor is desiring the lawful abstinence, since these refer to actions and attachments, not the higher world within. Virtue and abstinence consist in understanding and avoiding the inner causes of doubt; its action is to open the eyes of the heart and distinguish the essence of right from wrong.[7] To consume even a loaf of a forbidden bread (or to commit to any unjust act) will cause such a deep darkness that it would require years of repentance if one would wipe away such darkness from the heart. From a forbidden loaf rises forbidden deeds, and these engender spiritual destruction.[8]

It is narrated from Moses that he asked the Almighty Lord who were the dearest among His servants. And in his revelation he heard that the dearest among the Lord's servants were the abstinent ones, since they have closed the door of self-torment.

Sufis propound four rules regarding abstinence: to eat only what is lawful, and that not in excess; to control one's animal desires; to keep oneself away from deceptions, outwardly and inwardly; and to remain in this state until the last breath of life. In this way one remains abstinent and content until the final union with truth and reality takes place.[9]

The Koran teaches mankind that, "It is not your flesh and blood that reaches God but your piety that touches Him." (Koran: XXII, 37) Piety has three levels: on the apparent level, it consists in avoiding deception and degradation; on the inner level it has the sense of avoiding doubts in the heart; and at the intellectual level it has the meaning of keeping the mind unbound by the limitations and attachments of the world so that the spirit may ascend towards unity with the Divine. And indeed, this is the richest promise of the spiritual journey, the achievement of perfect piety that Sufis find in the inner heart. Throughout his life, the human being faces the threat of harm and destruction many times over, but if he is armored with the strength of piety he may be saved from all hardship and danger.[10] It has been narrated from Zunnun that, "Pious is he who does not contaminate his appearance with disputes and his heart with disgrace."[11] The greater the piety one has, the closer to reality one may approach.

CHAPTER FOUR

Sabr (Patience)

True lovers ponder not upon the bright array of others;
They are measured with the scales of patience.

Nirvan

Sabr may be understood as endurance and fortitude through the abandonment of impatience and complaint. In the language of Sufism patience represents the proper manner of awaiting the opening of the Divine. But this patient waiting is no simple matter.

Sabr has been divided into three categories: the patience of the common people in disciplining their *nafs*, the patience of the pious in working to benefit future generations, and the patience of the Sufis in avoiding the desires of the world. Some Sufis have said that one who is patient is grateful even in times of misfortune through perseverance in God.[1]

The disciplining of one's *nafs* is indispensable to the practice of patience, and this discipline is achieved through lessening the grip on the self of the chains of desires, while at the same time setting praiseworthy goals for one's life. Working to achieve those goals assists in striving to avoid low qualities and base manners, while advancing one's knowledge and skill so that one can become a valuable and peaceful member of the society. Such practices demand patience and inward dedication, but the rewards are rich: becoming an outstanding individual is helpful to one's own life as well to the betterment of other members of the human race. But it is not an easy task to be accomplished through good intentions alone. To the contrary, only through patience can the obstacles on the path of enlightenment be overcome.

A second category of patience is the patience of the pious. A pious individual is one who has already advanced himself above the rank of the common people. He has disciplined himself and already achieved praiseworthy goals. He has taken it upon himself to contribute to future generations, to think in advance of his times, and to educate himself accordingly. Preparing a suitable ground for the advancement of future generations demands patience as well as dedication and selflessness.

The third category of patience is the patience of the Sufis. A Sufi is one who is searching for unlimited understanding; remaining attracted to the desires of the world will prevent one from even appreciating the importance of the path of the Sufi. Thus to become a Sufi one necessary preparation is the freeing of the inner self from the imprisonment of the desires of the world, with the awareness such freedom does not lie in mortification, but only true inner freedom. Such freedom clears the ground for better thinking, living, and the attainment of a peaceful manner.

The author of the authoritative *Resaleh Ghosheiri* evokes the nuances of the patience of worshippers and the patience of lovers of the Divine. As he relates, the worshippers' patience is better kept and the lovers' patience better left.[2] One who is pious waits for God through his patience and worship, and so must be persistent. The lover is attracted toward God and cannot remain patient in his love since the heat of love so easily may dwindle into coldness.

The human being lives in the world of nature, and nature is filled with all the different colors, tastes, and dimensions. Pain and suffering, grief and sadness, comfort and good fortune do not spring like flowers from the soil; rather, they are all part of human life, and everyone will taste of them. Should we consider these events to be destiny, then it is a destiny that follows its course without consulting anyone! The individual should not fail and lose hope when misfortune knocks, nor should he forget the bounds of moderation when fortune blesses him. To remain firm on one's own path necessitates patience in conserving one's strength and will.[3] Indeed, it may be fairly said that it is the believer who meets the armada of destiny secure in the armor of patience. The (Koran: XXV, 75) provides us with the most succinct wisdom: it reads, "Those are the ones who will be rewarded with the highest place in heaven because of their patient constancy: Therein shall they be met with salvation and peace." Elsewhere: "Ye who believe, seek help with patient perseverance and prayer: for God is with those who patiently wait." (Koran: II, 153)

The individual who is impatient in enduring suffering and hardship is not well suited for thc path of Sufism. Sufis are the lovers of the truth of Being and are indifferent to the prospect of reward in achieving it. Whether or not they are given good fortune, as Sufis they seek knowledge and understanding of the rules of existence; they know that patience is a part of the achievement of such an understanding. Patience is the state of contentment with the destiny of Being. A Sufi knows that the world of existence is the domain of rules, and that no single particle acts unless in accordance with the rules of the eternal essence. A Sufi is aware in his understanding of the destination of Being. One who discovers the destination and the rules of this infinitely designed system that we call world remains steadfast at all times. He will not lose hope when misfortune occurs, and will not fall into smug self-satisfaction when fortune knocks.

Discovery and success come only through patience, but are not to be thought of as rewards for patience. Sufis live patiently for the Divine; they do not love God because He rewards them with the benefits of life, but because He is to be loved. Since He is the source of that eternal knowledge, those who are attracted toward knowledge will embrace the Beloved within their whole being. Whether or not the road toward the beloved is filled with hardship or paved with ease, such incidentals will not alter their intention and dedication: quite simply, they know that they must achieve their goal.

It is told that once a group of people came to Shebli, an ancient Sufi, and assured him that they were his devotees. Shebli picked up a rock and threw it at them—in consternation they all ran away. Shebli shouted, "If you are my friends, why are you running away from my hardship?"[4] This wise and wry gesture represents a discipline among Sufis. They do not run away from hardship; as the lovers of truth they accept and trust whatever comes from truth, instead of arguing, rejecting, and denying truth.

The world is not all comfort and wealth: pain follows ease, poverty descends from wealth, and richness is bought with hardship. Since the world is a house of change, pain and suffering have the upper hand in the fear of insecurity and doubt, while comfort and ease presuppose a stability that is not to be found within the confines of the world.[5]

The author of *Sufi Nameh* suggests several modalities of patience. One is to keep oneself away from desires and through patient learning master the discipline of life. This is proper patience for beginners and for followers, who must of necessity first close the doors of passion and persist in patience until their heart reaches the light of guidance. Koran: II, 155, reads that, "Be sure, We shall test you with something of fear and hunger." Next is to endure those pains and hardships that arise out of the faults of others; here we have the model of saints who were patient with all.

The life stories of the prophets and Sufis evoke the value of patience. Noah, Zakarra, Abraham, Moses, and Jesus all were put to test and were told to "persevere in patience and constancy." Prophet Mohammad suffered much hardship from his enemies yet he was instructed to "await in patience the command of thy Lord" (Koran: LII, 48).[6]

The rules and laws of Being suggest that everything must undergo the test of hardship if anything is to develop and progress toward perfection. Indeed, the very history of civilization shows that it is only through endurance that the fittest survive. Whoever shall endure hardship becomes strong: as Nietzsche sagely wrote, "what does not kill me, makes me stronger".

Comfort and pain are reflections of each other; patience is the key in understanding both. A Sufi takes patience with him as a friend to assist him in leaving behind the cares of the world. Since it cannot be denied that everything comes from the Divine, thus He is the source of all knowledge for Sufis (and indeed for all knowledge of any kind), whether in times of fortune or misfortune. Such events that we may call ill or fortunate are only words that we apply to the ephemeral; the Sufi patiently seeks the permanent. "Is not God enough for His servant?" (Koran: XXXIX, 36) Truly, an individual who is ripe for the path of understanding must ask himself if it is not the Divine alone who has brought him forth from the eternity of infinity into worldly existence, and yet again that same God who beckons him forth once more toward eternity and infinity in such a way that not a single fiber of his body could resist. Thus, just as pain is a condition of life, patience is a cure for that condition through its very essence.

Constant change is the rule of the world of nature; in it fortune and misfortune are like the seasons of the year, transient in their course as one replaces another, ephemeral in their effects, like the snows of winter that melt beneath the warmth of spring. Primitive peoples govern their lives and worship their gods according to the seasons; with wisdom the mind may learn to remain patient in times of hardship, since like the winter snow the face of pain will finally disappear, revealing beneath it the profile of patience that will remain.

Like piety, patience as it is practiced in Sufism possesses both an outwardly apparent and inwardly essential aspect. A *salek* always thinks before he speaks, awaiting the opportune moment, so as not to say what he may well later regret; likewise, he constantly attends to the care of his body and mind so as not to fall into distress and helplessness; most important of all, he keeps his heart from falling into rejection and denial: perhaps the most difficult of tests. Weakness in patience reflects uncertainty of belief, since patience is one of the reasons and methods that keeps belief intact.[7] It has been narrated from Amir-al-Moumenin Ali that the relationship between patience and belief is like to that of mind and body: a body without mind will not live; belief without patience will not endure.

A believer strives to become learned, familiar with the rules of reality and the laws of the Divine. For a believer, God is all mercy and kindness: and so any event follows through His logic. To understand Divine logic, the believer waits and remains in patience and avoids hasty and imbalanced reactions. Prophet Mohammad said in the *Hadith* that there is that which you like but which is not to your benefit, but that there is also that which you dislike but which benefits you. Here the Prophet offers us an invitation to the understanding of the wisdom that lies behind events, either fortunate or unfortunate in their outward and immediate manifestation. Patience is a quality which comes after the quality of *faghr* (poverty) and it arises from belief. A Sufi must be a person of knowledge; he is aware that all the events of the world of matter arise as events out of the operation of meaningful laws and rules. And so he may remain patient in his suffering and thankful in his joy until he learns the rules of Divinity, and then there shall remain no impermanence within him to lie under the shadow of fear, of greed, or of ignorance.

There remains another way of usefully categorizing patience, in terms of its relation to the different elements of the being of the individual. Here it is possible to speak of the patience of the *nafs*; the patience of the heart; and the patience of the soul.[8] The patience of *nafs* consists in perseverance in performing religious duties, and remaining steadfast in times of pain as well as in those of comfort. The patience of the heart lies in persistence in the purifying of one's intentions, and a like persistence in meditation and remembering the Almighty Lord. The patience of the soul consists in persistence in witnessing the Eternal beauty with the help of insight. Among the highest of the unities that underlie the different varieties of patience is patience with and through God, since such patience comes after the annihilation.

As well, patience may be divided into three levels. There is patience at the time of temptation, when one tries to keep away from the forbidden no matter how delightfully alluring it might appear. Above that is patience at the time of worship, which has the sense of grateful worship of God without expectation of reward; this is the best type of worship that may be expected from a person of limited mind. Finally, there is patience during misfortune that consists in waiting until the misfortune passes, since nothing on the face of nature can last forever.[9]

It is said that patience walks hand in hand with intellect, each supporting the other. The more intellect one possesses, the more one may understand the meaning of patience and the essential logic behind it. Knowledge is the soul and the patience the body; the foundation of both is intellect.

Moses asked Almighty God to let him know the way to gain His approbation. He heard in response, "You, the son of Omran, My pleasure with you is when you remain satisfied with My Destiny."[10] Moulana Shah Maghsoud has stated that for those who obey the powers of their intellect, destiny is nothing but the will of their being. Those powers of intellect consist in the understanding of the logic of the universe, and the Divine wisdom that underlies it. If there is such wisdom, the human being has definitely his own proper share of it, however imperfectly he might make use of it. Imam Ali says,"You think of yourself as a small body, nay, a greater world is folded in you. You are the Clear Book in which every word sheds light upon a new secret." One who knows remains satisfied, and one who knows not keeps a counterfeit in the place of the original truth, and searches for the truth outside of his being.

Satisfaction with His destiny is the highest rank of reliance upon Him, since satisfaction comes from the heart, the center of life, the House of the Divine, the origin of cognition. Satisfaction is the peace of heart in knowing the wisdom of Being and the agreement of heart with whatever He approves of and chooses.[11] Zunnun, one of the great Sufis, says a true servant is one who remains the servant of God at all times, as God remains always one's God.

The Prophet Mohammad said, "If you do not see Him yet you know that He sees you." That is the knowledge of the believer who is aware of God's intimate closeness. Conversely, one may not know the rules of Being, yet one has no choice but to measure one's gait according to them. The maker, the rule, the follower, and the enforcer are all the same: the eternal Being that is the Divine. The more advanced a being is in his understanding, the broader are the bounds of what he can learn and know. That is what reliance on God means. The heart of the abstinent is fortified because of reliance; the heart of the reliant is enriched through approval, and the heart of a Sufi flourishes because of contentment. Thus a Sufi does not look to hardship and comfort, but rather searches for the Giver of all as is his quest.

Rumi says:

Job was patient for seven years,
For all the misfortunes he had received.
During all that time of suffering,
He prayed and was thankful to God.
One day he heard in a revelation:
"I have given patience to every part of you.
Do not look proudly at your patience.
You see but your patience,
See instead the Giver of patience."[12]

Hardship and ease, misfortune and good-fortune are all the reflections of one another; they pass across the stage of life but for a while. They play their requisite parts and then disappear. One who has the whole picture and knows the whole story remains steadfast in his intentions and manner. Transient reflections will not become the source of his being, and thus do not play the essential part in his life. He is patient in his quest for knowledge and remains strong until he achieves his goal.

A heart, as Hazrat Mir Ghotbeddin says, which is amused, busied, and impatient with notions of "more" and "less", is not a heart but a stomach.[13] In our impatience, how often should we reflect upon this truth?

CHAPTER FIVE

Sedgh (Truthfulness)

*Only those who can keep their inner identity away
from the imaginary motivations of human nature are
truthful in their heart.*

Psalms of Gods

Sedgh signifies truthfulness and honesty, but the concept
of *sedgh* embodies a much more complex conception than
just the ordinary idea of an honest man as opposed to a liar.
More deeply, an honest person is one whose actions and
promises agree with his inner intentions and thoughts, so that
he is as he presents himself to be.[1] Truthfulness is thus a
foundation for actions and behavior. Moral intentions are
perfected into action through and by such a basis and foundation.

Honesty in everyday life consists in the agreement between intention and behavior, easing individual life and con-
tributing to social well-being and thus to the advancement of
human civilization. To the extent that honesty is practiced by
all, people face far fewer difficulties and everyone's rights are
understood and respected. In the case of the individual, instead of spending time and effort to make lies appear as
truths, and so adding to the suspiciousness of everyone, his
time can be better used more wisely. In a hypothetical society
where all transactions are based on honesty, all would be
worthy of respect and trust. A dishonest person who misrep-
resents his intentions cannot be worthy of trust, and such an
individual's life becomes permeated by an atmosphere of
dishonesty, so that all of his actions, even those which are
well-intentioned, will lead not to the straight path and the
direct understanding of reality, but rather into the morass of

destruction. The rules of harmony and cooperation do not permit the dishonest to progress along the path of spirituality, however hard they may strive.

The honest person is one who possesses both outwardly apparent and inwardly sanctified sincerity and truthfulness.[2] His honesty does not consist in merely telling the truth, but in the inner character that makes the telling of truth possible. A person with a fundamentally unclean character, even if he attempts to be honest, cannot truly ever be so, since inner truthfulness remains closed to such an individual.

It is narrated from Juneid, who is among the greatest of Sufis, that an honest man is one who speaks truly when only a lie can save him.[3] Ostad Abu Ali says that, truthfulness is to be what you pretend to be and pretend what you really are.[4]

"Now I pray to God that you should do no evil: not that we should appear approved, but that you should do that which is honest, though we be as reprobates. For we can do nothing against the truth, but only for the truth." (Corinthians, 13:7 - 8)

The Almighty Lord says, "God may reward the people of truth for their truth..." (Koran: XXXIII, 24) And according to the rule of harmony one receives whatever one deserves or provides for one's self.

Honesty is a rule that should govern action by defining and cleansing the essential self from which all moral action springs. Seen negatively, if honesty does not accompany an action, then that action is a deception that leads towards destruction.[5] It is written in *Sufi Nameh* that the Almighty Lord called upon them (all beings) to the covenant of servitude and said "Am I not your Lord?" (Koran: VII, 172): All, good or wicked, honest or dishonest, fortunate or miserable, confessed that, "Yes, we do so testify that you are the Lord." (Koran: VII, 172) All claimed to be truthful, since honesty and the lie seemed equal at the time the claim was made. But when the reality of loyalty and rectitude appeared, truthfulness fell into the world of the material, and some remained truthful to that testimony while others abandoned their testimony and so became liars. The people of the truth are those who are saved; the liars are condemned to their lies. The Prophet Mohammad ordered his disciples to be truthful and honest always, since truthfulness directs the spirit toward goodness.[6] One who is inwardly and not merely outwardly truthful, whatever he receives, is thus sprung from truthfulness; the whole of his being is governed by the rule of agreement.

The signs of truthfulness are seen when one keeps one's intentions, deeds, thoughts, and actions all in agreement with each other. Rectitude, which is the light of the heart, will flow from the heart into speech and the saying of truth will manifest the intentions of the heart. As was narrated from the Prophet Mohammad, "The tongue and the heart of a believer are in accord." The truthfulness of word and heart will reveal honesty in actions—and all will assist in the performance of truthful worship.[7]

Sufis believe that a believer must be honest in his devotion, if he is not ignorant, for dishonest actions will end badly. A believer must truthfully welcome his master's advice, so that his honesty and the master's acceptance accompany his steps towards understanding. The blessing of honesty saves the faithful from the ruin wrought by the world, and cleanses the humble clay of desires from the doorway of the heart so that the radiance of spirituality may shine within.[8]

Sheikh Ahmad Ja'am, (a twelfth century Sufi) wrote: "Many people hear the verses of the Holy Book. Some will fall into ecstasy and some into falseness. Yet the verses are the same: whether they merely hear or really listen separates them. The truthful heart listens to the truth; the false heart only hears falsehood."[9]

An ill heart cannot listen to the truth, just as a sick body may not enjoy fine food. If a man be sick, he needs to find a cure, not a recipe. One who is healthy does not lose the taste for dining, yet if he seeks the joy of good food while he is sick, he only wastes delicacies better lavished on the healthy. He seeks only disgrace and tastes only his inner sickness. But one who is healthy can enjoy even the blandest meal, in the knowledge that he derives nourishment from it.[10] The follower of the way of Sufism must strive for health, and the nurturing of the fundamentally healthy, and not for persuasion of the weak and sick of spirit. With this in mind, Sufis have divided people into categories such as: the prophets, who are the best and most knowledgeable of the creation; the believers, the honest ones, and the Sufis, who are the dearest creations of the two worlds; the inwardly dishonest whose destiny is in the deepest of hell; and the infidels whose essence is ignorance, who are almost inevitably misled, and who are the dwellers of hell.[11]

The seekers and the believers of reality live honestly in their hearts. Their ears are tuned to the sublime magnetic waves of the eternal existence of Being; their lives are lived in harmony with the rules of the existence. They see, hear, and witness reality as it really is, the reality that must always be hidden from the hearts of the ignorant. Thus, the honest heart lives according to the unchangeable rules of the existence, the rules of eternity, of infinity, of Being. Those who are slaves of their own passions and desires cannot live in their hearts, and the hearts of the aware are illuminated by the light of the infinite rules that spring from the Divine.

The saved are not misled by the deceit of the *nafs*, of changeable and transient nature, nor are they misled into listening to any voice that is not of the eternal Being.[12] Only those who can listen to the truth can understand and so enjoy truth.

Hafez, one of the great Persian Sufi poets, wrote that,

"On the road to the house of Leili, the beloved,
Lie many dangers.
Yet the first condition of taking a step
Is to be Majnun, the lover."[13]

One of the essential preconditions of devotion toward the direction of understanding, the goal of a *salek*, is the honesty of the heart. When the novice, through the instruction of the teacher (who is rarer than the phoenix and cannot be found among the traders in the marketplace of any religion) begins to polish his heart and rub away the deceit of the changeable accretions of nature, revealing in their place stability and constancy in the house of heart, his heart becomes receptive to the subtlest waves of spirituality. This reception and transference of knowledge is the reason why Sufis say that spiritual knowledge is transferred from heart to heart—and not from mind to mind.

Mind, or its physical vessel, the brain, is the receiver of influences which are visible and perceivable by and through the senses insofar as their inherent limitations permit. The conditions for receiving those perceptions are the health of the brain and the organs of the senses. The heart is the receiver of those influences which are invisible (and may feel as pain or cramp only in times of deep distress) to the senses. Heart receives those subtle waves, influences that are on a different level of frequency, one usually hidden from the attention of the senses. The organs of sense understand only those readily apparent events which happen within the borders of common perception. Yet though the senses may be dulled, the heart perceives a different level of waves within a different border and frequency. We should remember that if science still has no definitive stamp of approval for such an understanding, it is only because the scientific method is still bound to a primitive level compared to the possibilities for spiritual advancement that have been known for centuries. And if science has not yet found approval for such an advanced level of understanding, that does not imply that spiritual revelation is in any way inadequate: to the contrary, such a difference in understanding only exposes the materialist bias of science with all its limitations.

Truer wisdom may be found in the Koran, which says that the heart will not lie on what it sees; and Sufis direct the attention of their devotees to the center of the heart. There are practices in Sufism that discover and comprehend conditions through which concentrations of the energies of the senses in the heart may allow the heart to see, hear, and discover truth without being bound by the limitations of the organs of senses as they exist. But those instructions are a private teaching not given to general practices. Those who are privileged to receive these private practices are the few true devoted students of Sufism. Moulana Shah Maghsoud spoke authoritatively: "When the energies of your senses, altogether, gather in your heart and do not wish to return, then you will find your 'self'. When your Being is nourished by the center of life, you will discover the illuminated face of your 'self'."[14] With his wisdom he instructed his followers that, "You shall gather and return the scattered energies of the senses to your heart. Remain there, all peaceful and concentrated, and manifest the luminous figure of your 'self'. If it breathes onto the elements of your being from the Eternal Soul, then you will step out of the realm of death."[15]

A Sufi is able to see his true identity. His surroundings are not the dreary realm of ignorance and loss, where the multitude dwell in fitting darkness. The individual who seeks truth must be inwardly truthful in his essence and so in his quest; in practice, he must always work to keep the channel between his heart and mind open: thus he remains a monotheist; his mind, intentions, and thoughts remain in harmony with his quest and actions.

In remaining truthful to himself and to his quest, the *salek* must be careful in his associations, and cultivate the purity of his heart free from the encroachments of the ignorant. "Remember that the lie does not know the truth, that wickedness is unaware of mercy, that cruelty does not realize justice."[16] It is only the honest devotion which rises from the heart, and it is not imprisoned by the two worlds of the earth and the eternal heavens. It is narrated from Abu Ali Roodbari, an ancient Sufi, that "If Paradise were to tell you that the heavenly doors pour forth gifts, what would you wish to have given to you? I should say, nothing except the Beloved: the Truth, the Divine."[17]

Thus, honesty directs the pious seeker toward purification and away from whatever corrupts and so impedes the passage toward reality and the realization of the spiritual quest. The rules propounded allow the *salek* to give up the deceit of the world, to put the body into servitude, to present life to the Divine, and to become free from the desires of the world. I would ask you to remember well, that if an individual seeks a reward for his devotion, he is not pious but merely a business person. One can reach the stages of certainty only if one guards the principles of religion from heresy.

Worship that is not inspired by the honesty of heart and ecstasy of life is either motivated by greed for the profits of the world or for the desire for the blessings of Paradise. Yet those few who have possessed great insight have said that the world is forbidden for the people of futurity, and futurity is forbidden for the people of the world; both are forbidden for the people of God. Hazrat Mir Ghotbeddin Mohammad Angha says that people of the Divine have cast the desires of the two worlds out of their hearts; thus their hearts beat only for the Divine.

I would ask you, for whom does your heart beat? You are directed towards that beloved.

CHAPTER SIX

Safa (Purity)

For those who purify their hearts for forty days,
The springs of knowledge will flow
From their hearts to their lips.
                                                    Sacred Hadith

The pure is the opposite of the contaminated, and for mankind purity is attained by the avoidance of indecency. According to *tasawouf,* purity has a pillar and a branch. The pillar of purity is the separation of the heart from anything but truth, and the branch for this pillar is the practice of remaining in solitude apart from the treacherous world, the world of change.[1]

A Sufi is not the slave to desires that might be tempted by the material world. Some say that those enlightened individuals were called Sufis because of the *safa* (purity) in their hearts. That is to say, those wise ones were called Sufis because they purified their being completely, and kept their hearts away from the temptations of the world.[2] It is narrated from Sahl ibn Abdullah al Tustari that a Sufi is one who is cleansed of impurity, is always in the state of meditation, and in whose eyes gold and clay are of equal value.[3]

Many great Sufi scholars have stressed the importance of purity in attaining and binding together the other principles that a *salek* must observe. Ghosheiri, the twelfth century Persian Sufi and scholar, wrote that one who truly worships God must not associate anything with his worship,[4] in other words, his worship must be purified of anything that is not God. Such a truthful individual does not fall into the trap of popular praise in his worship, since the goal of his worship is closeness to God rather than any honors from the people.

Abu Ali Daghagh said that the sincere do not listen to people's praise, while the truthful avoid the desires of the *nafs*.[5] Zunnun has said that if sincerity is not accompanied by patience and truthfulness, it remains incomplete. According to Juneid, there is a secret held just between the Lord of the universe and His human servants, and this secret is sincerity: even the angels do not know this secret and have not written of it, nor does the devil know this secret to destroy it, and desire does not know of it to influence it.[6] Sincerity is reached when a person sees always Divine as his witness. Yet not all worshippers are pure and sincere, and not all those who perform their prayers are properly respectful.

It is said that the witnessing of reality can be likened to the date palm, which only grows in a warm climate and then only in suitable soil. It will not grow in a cold atmosphere, nor in stony ground. Likewise, witnessing the truth of Being requires the soil of a pure heart, love, and knowledge, until after tender cultivation, servitude blossoms into respect and sincerity.[7] And it is therefore to remember that not all prayers are accepted, nor all words said in truth: nor are all trees palms. To witness in a heart that is not purified from duality and hypocrisy may be likened to the fate of the palm tree in a cold climate: although it may grow, it will never blossom nor yield its fruit.

Moulana Shah Maghsoud said that the blessing is received through the teachings of the masters of hearts, in the merit of servitude, and by following the footsteps of the great masters, without the temptations of the immature intellect.[8] This blessing will open the pure heart and so illuminate the inner self; and only then does an individual even deserve to repent and purify his nature. The servitude of the pure is based upon their devotion and sincerity. They avoid the desires of the *nafs* and are present at the solitude of the great masters. Sheikh Ahmad Ja'am writes that only believers whose witnessing is accompanied by sincerity are accepted by the Divine. These individuals are free from doubt, heresy, and hypocrisy.[9] They are, thus, believers among the worshippers whose unification is real; their sustenance is love, their chariot is virtue, they rely on God; they are honest, their bridle is submission, and the illumination of their heart is brighter than the light of the sun.

The light of understanding arises from the heart of such believers. The rays of this light reflect not only the earth, the sky, the heaven, the angels, the celestial space, and all of creation, but also reflect from the heart of the knower onto the known, onto God. God will clarify this light, robe it with the honored mantle of approval, and perfume it with the breeze of unification. The roots of this light are firm and its branches reach upward into heaven. Its root is in the heart of the Sufi and its branches are in the House of Glory.[10] Divine grace nourishes this light and permits its owner to drink from the Wine of friendship served in the Cup of love. Such an illumination reveals the Divine secrets to the Sufi, the owner of heart.

Once someone asked the Prophet Mohammad for advice about performing his prayers. The Prophet answered, "Draw the light of sincerity into your heart, so that on the day of resurrection you will not have to be questioned about your deeds, since the Almighty Lord asks for sincerity and not the motions of the body."[11] Yet there are many who worship God out of mere habit and custom; they are not among the pure and sincere, and they do no more than mechanical obeisance to God through their prayers. The imitation of others is for the ignorant, who dwell in the realm of not-knowing, a realm proper for destruction, not worship.

The basis for understanding reality and so being able to sincerely worship God is laid through seeking and acquiring the light of knowledge. The message of the prophets is an invitation to the people to make their hearts pure and sincere. Hypocrisy, agitation, selfishness, and egotism are traits of character that lead an individual back into the deepest darkness of desire and deprive him of the heaven of understanding. The student must be sincere in his servitude or else his service cannot be accepted by any teacher.[12] Sincerity is not to be found in fasting or sitting in loneliness doing nothing, but rather reflects that purity of body and soul which is the key to receiving revelation.

But if someone has an essentially impure heart, the doors of knowledge will never open to him, even should he strive for forty years.[13] It is not fitting for such individuals who are inwardly unclean and poor in spirit to even attempt to journey along the path of spirituality, lest they defile it with their impure footsteps. The door of understanding is best closed to them.

Yet all who are not born saints have some impurities within the heart, contaminants which can be removed through practice so that the individual may properly embark upon the path of spirituality without committing impiety. One of the most basic practices of Sufism is this purification of the heart. The heart is the center of life, a strong magnetic power within the body. When the heart is freed from the pollution of earthly desires and all that is base and ignoble, it may then attract similar harmonious qualities, and so enrich itself. Just as like attracts like, so too the perishable world attracts desires for the perishable world, and weak spirits attract further weakness to themselves.

One of the reasons why heart has been likened to a mirror in Sufism is that one's whole being is reflected in it. A shining clean mirror shows reality as clearly as it actually is, while a dirty mirror reflects dirt, and shows nothing but a broken image of what is unknown. When the heart is pure, it deserves to see reflected in itself the face of the Beloved. Such purity is achieved when there remain no traces of worldly desires, nor inclinations toward anything other than the light of reality which will shine and be reflected in the mirror of the heart. One must remember that worldly desires are but traps that limit the human being to a narrow, impoverished world. As should the individual become entrapped by the chains of such attractions, he can only walk in chains under the shadow of the governor of darkness, and all his goals remain under the dominion of that master.

The striving for illumination of the heart is beyond any language or any limited system of logic. It may not be defined. It arises from the well-spring of love, since only the lovers of reality stride freely across the path of understanding.

Rumi says,

"First cleanse yourself of the dust,
Then wait until you shall see the light."

If the sight of the heart is blinkered by worldly attachments, then one simply must strive to wipe out this darkness in order to see the light. The only alternative is to dwell forever in the darkness.

One will see through insight
Just as much as he purifies his heart.
He who polishes more,
Sees more, and the image is seen in its clarity.[14]

A believer is always aware of the mercy, the grace, and the gift of Being. Nothing but the Divine should engage the inner heart of a believer in truth: and he shall wait until the cloud of prosperity gathers, the winds of mercy blow, the lightning of repentance strikes, the thunder of kindness roars, and the rain of knowledge pours forth, and the light of understanding shines.[15]

The story of life in the world has two chapters: It begins with love for the world and ends with eternal death and destruction, writes Moulana Shah Maghsoud in his *Nirvan.* The life of the many is essentially limited by these conditions, for such is their essence. There appear no signs of real generosity or magnanimity in their lives, which are indeed an expenditure from a small and diminishing fund of existence that they hoard as long as they can. And so their desires are nothing more than the heralds of their death. Nirvan, the incarnation of Perfect Purity, finds the truth of Being in the abandonment of desires. Until the attainment of complete salvation and eternal life he is bound to wear the raiment of death and struggle along the paths of life that lead nowhere. He will kindle the light of his heart through the power of abstaining from the pleasures of the world, aided by the purification of meditation in solitude. "...Nirvan's wealth is Being, and it rests within his soul and within the purity of his heart."[16]

CHAPTER SEVEN

Vud (Love)

Should the cup of love turn, it would burn the universe,
It would smash into pieces this pillarless world.
The world becomes ocean, the ocean evaporates,
And there remains no man to survive.
Then the heavens open up, dimensions dissolve,
Universe falls into ecstasy, and ecstasy into despair.
Attar (thirteenth century Persian Sufi)

Vud means *eshgh* and *eshgh* derives from the word ashaghe, which refers to a red vine that grows upon another plant, twisting about it and feeding itself from that plant until its host eventually yellows and dies. The metaphor paradoxically, in its gruesomeness, expresses the truth of an all-consuming love that empties the lover of all earthly qualities, for *eshgh* also grows and nurtures itself upon the lover. But for love to be praiseworthy it must have as its object a beloved worthy of praise.

The lover is the Sufi, the Beloved, the Divine, and love dwells within the seeking heart of the Sufi. It is said that love is a fire that God kindles in the hearts of His servants, where it burns and so consumes all the curtains of separation and the veils of ignorance in their hearts.

Let love exist,
No fear if I exist or not.
To become pure,
Gold should rise from the fire.[1]

Love has been likened to Wine, where the Wine bearer is the Divine, the Beloved, that pours the ecstasy of love for the sake of purification into the cup of heart so that the Sufi becomes drunken from its burning illumination.

> I heard an inspiration while in the Winery,
> "Drink Wine, if you desire to be forgiven."[2]

Love is that strong magnetic power that connects all the particles of the universe together. The basic principles, the beginning, the end, and the discovery of what is secret, are all founded on the pillar of *eshgh*. Creation and all its creatures are the outcome of love. Love is the bond that binds the book of creation together.

Throughout the world of Sufism, love is an eternal theme which Sufis in all eras have gracefully glorified in delicate poetry. After all, it is love that purifies, concentrates, brings beauty, and makes the pillars of the universe strong. To the Sufi,

> God is love, Prophet is love, Religion is love,
> From the smallest grain of sand to the highest heavens,
> All are but wrapped in love.

Existence is based on love and as existence has levels and stages, so does love. At every stage and level love has a different manifestation, each with its own beauty.

Love has a rebellious nature; it will not rest until it robs the lover of his being, unless it receives the guardianship and companionship of the intellect and wisdom. This intellectual power works as an ordering force that directs the spiritual traveller toward a favorable destination. Since the road to knowledge is a long path hedged by many dangers, without the chariot of love no one could find the energy and drive to continue towards such a distant destiny.

A *salek* cultivates the seed of love in his heart through his eagerness for knowledge; he thus steps into the field of exploration, connecting his life to the magnetic power of love radiating from the heart of the Master, and reflecting the Divine love. The power that gently touches and guides the direction of the *salek*'s life comes from within the chest of the Master and is a divine manifestation. Through this connection, the *salek* begins to travel on the path of Divinity; without it, nothing good will come to the *salek*, and any experience that he has will be but the image of illusion and imagination.

Amir-al-Moumenin Ali says: "The Almighty Lord offers a Wine (referring to the verse 21 in Sura LXXVI of Koran, which says: 'Their Lord will give them to drink of a Wine, pure and holy') to His teachers (His people) that when they drink, they shall become drunken; while drunken, they shall become clean; while clean, they shall annihilate; while they are annihilating, they shall become pure; when pure, they shall strive; when they strive, they shall find; and when they reach forth into unity, then there shall remain no separation between them and their Beloved."[3]

Some Sufis believe that the love cultivated by faith is the original love, as the Koran (II, 160) reads that "And those who believe love God more strongly."

Belief and love both develop in the heart, and the heart is the House of Eternal knowledge; as the Prophet said: "Consult your heart and hear the secret ordinance of God, discovered by the inward knowledge of the heart which is faith and Divinity." A believer who has received Divine light sees by that light. The individual who truly knows God can walk on water, and mountains will move at his command.

Attar Neyshapouri writes in his *Mantegh-al-Teyr* about the stages of the heart. He relates love to the second stage and says in a beautiful poem that the valley of love comes after the valley of quest. He writes:

"Then comes the valley of love;
Whoever enters this valley, falls into fire.
The lover becomes alike to that fire:
Warm, hot, and rebellious;

The Good and the bad become equal to him.
When love arrives, everything perishes.
Others live for a promised tomorrow,
But the lover lives in his own presence.
The intellect loses significance,
Since love is not an art for the mind.
If your eyes may see secrets,
You will witness the origin.
But if your eyes are those of the mind,
You will not see even the image of love."[4]

Only those whose hearts are truly alive are able to pass the boundaries of love. In its highest form, pure love is reserved for those who have perfected themselves by passing through the successive stages of perfection. In its final perfection, love does not allow for any distance between the self and the Beloved; the "I" loses its significance. Such deep love brings the devotee to the final stage of annihilation where nothing remains of the seeker but the Beloved. In ascending to this level, love purifies the *salek*, preventing him from seeing any other than the Beloved. Through this annihilation, the Sufi will be lifted up in resurrection, for resurrection is the confession, and he will be reborn as the Essential Existence, and so will be honored through rebirth as a child of the spirit. Through this divine annihilation, his qualities become those of the Divine. Attaining union with the Essential Existence, he himself becomes the rule instead of the perceiver of the rule.

But this final annihilation is not to be quickly found: It is said that patience will not cure love, but that the impatient will not survive love. Love may be divided into two general levels; the beginner experiences the level of striving, while the pure possess the level of witnessing. The beginnings of spiritual love are fraught with the pain of heavy burdens and suffering of the heart, while the pure attain the wealth of witnessing the Beloved and the enjoyments of Divine Unity.[5]

Sheikh Ahmad Ja'am writes that love is the blessing of God, and like a wild bird that will only build its nest in a special place, so also love will not reside just anyplace, or make friends with just anyone. Love resembles guidance, cognition and wisdom, in that God gives these only to whomever He desires.[6] It has been narrated from the Prophet Mohammad that, "When God fills the hearts of His servants with His love, they will only be occupied with the thought of God. And the Creator will add to the joys and blessings of the remembrance held in them till He shall uncover eternal friendship for them and let fall the curtain between Him and them. These individuals who are chosen never forget God as all the others do. Their words will become like the words of the prophets. It is through such individuals that God may change destiny."[7]

Time and again in Sufism—in poetry, art, and learned scholarship—the treasure of love has been likened to fire: it burns and through such burning longing it purifies and illuminates. To the ignorant, it might seem a paradox that anyone would want to be burned, no matter how bright the resulting illumination might be. Today, many sects promise to provide the direct experience of divine love, quickly and painlessly, and the ignorant flock to them. The seeming paradox contained in the metaphor of fire expresses the truth of search for reality. If fire did not burn, neither would it purify and illuminate.

Sheikh Najmeddin Razi writes that love has the quality of fire and travels in the realm of nonexistence. The fire of love is directed toward unification and wherever it radiates, the intellect must yield up its house.[8] While the intellect is engaged in the process of building both the physical and spiritual worlds for its benefit, the burning fire of love is engaged in destroying both of these worlds. The intellect teaches nobility, but love purifies the kingdom.[9]

Divine love will not rest until it purifies the *salek* from all impurities that he may carry with himself on the path of spirituality. When such a light falls upon the being of lover, it illuminates and through such illumination the *salek* steps out of the darkness of ignorance. Then, from the midst of such purification, and the destruction of all of the dross of the material world, there arises a Man, a perfect *insan* (human being). Desires no longer attract him, as he has been purified by love. Blasphemy, sin, and corruption will together vanish through such purification. They are like the dew drops that vanish with the rising sun. The heat of love is to the short-comings of the lover like the rays of the sun to dew.[10]

When Divine love glows brighter in the heart of a believer, no other love can compete with it; as the Beloved, God has no rivals. Such an individual becomes a saint among saints; pure among the pure; and dear among dear hearts who take the path of spirituality. The grace of this love between the *salek* and God is unique. Whoever adds to it, becomes himself greater and draws closer to Divinity. A friend to God sees nothing but Him, chooses no one but Him, walks but towards Him, hears only Him, for He becomes the reason of life.[11]

It is narrated from the Prophet Mohammad that "Whoever would look on God, God looks towards, and whoever keeps his distance from the Divine, so Divinity keeps His distance from."[12] "Divine friendship will not be decreased by oppression nor increased by fidelity."[13]

It has come into *Hadith* that God says:

"Whoever would despise My saints is My enemy. And I choose my friends from among those who perform *nafeleh* (prayer of the lover of God). When I choose My friends, I will become their sight and their hearing, and I will give them victory over all."

For one filled with desires, love is a wish that, once granted, is no more.[14] And so those who claim to love God, yet only love Him in times of good fortune, do not love God at all. They love their own desire for fortune; and God forbids his love from entering the hearts of those pledged to others, said David, one of the Kings of Israel.[15]

Rabia, one of the greatest Sufis, has been narrated as saying: "Oh, my Lord, the stars are shining and the eyes of the people are closed; the Kings have shut their gates, and every lover is alone with his beloved: here I am alone with Thee." Rabia has been quoted as praying that: "Oh God, if I worship You in fear of Hell, burn me in Hell; if I worship You in the hope of Paradise, exclude me from Paradise. But if I worship You for You, withhold not Your everlasting Beauty from me."

Those who are drawn by Divine love fall into two groups. First are those who receive Divinity directly and without the need for a medium; they are prophets whose being naturally accepts the light of direct Divine guidance. The second group is formed of the apostles and saints who receive the blessing of Divine love through their devotion and with the help of the prophets.[16]

Love ultimately may take the step into annihilation and thus unite the lover with the Beloved; this the intellect cannot do, for while the intellect has its proper objects. The Almighty Lord is not the object of the intellect and so cannot be perceived by through it[17]: "No vision can grasp Him, but His grasp is over all vision." (Koran: VI, 103) and, "Nor shall they compass aught of His knowledge except as He willeth." (Koran: II, 155)

Reasoning based on the perceptions of the senses or rationalism founded on a closed system of mental logic possess no way toward Him, and so a seeker does not attempt to reach Him through the guidance of the intellect. Rather, the proper direction is to be found through the guidance of love.

"The friend conquered me completely,
I am only a name and the rest is Him."[18]

It has been written that the people of the *zekr* have four levels: some are in the level of desires, some are in the level of servitude, and others are in the level of love. The fourth level is that of Ascension. The spirit of a spiritual traveler will not ascend until he is in this stage.

In the first level, the *salek* is apparently in solitude. He performs the *zekr* only through words, while his heart is yet busied by other things.[19] During the second level, as the *salek* performs the *zekr* he tries to be present in his heart, but on occasion his heart strays elsewhere; yet he persists and studies hard to keep his heart present at all times. Most of the people of the *zekr* may be placed in this level.

At the third level, the *zekr* by itself covers and fills the whole heart and the performer remembers his *zekr* always. He prefers to remain in the solitude of his heart, rather than busying himself with matters that do not have spiritual value. This is the stage of closeness, and only a few reach this level. The closeness reflects the *salek*'s growing understanding of Divinity. In this stage, the *zekr*, that is the remembrance of the Beloved, fills the heart; during the fourth stage the Beloved fills the heart of the Sufi. And of course there is a difference between the one who only knows the name of the Beloved and the one who is united with the Beloved. There are times when the lover is so saturated by the Beloved that he forgets all else.

When someone speaks, he is on the level of desire; when his wish is surpassed, the level is called devotion. When devotion waxes strong, it is called affection; and extreme affection is called love. When this spiritual passenger of Divine love comes to your heart, honor it. Empty the house of your heart for this love, since love will tolerate no rival.[20]

Love is at once the chariot of travellers and the carriage of followers. It burns the wisdom of fifty years in a moment and so purifies the owner. Whatever an acolyte may find in a hundred *chellehs* (spiritual purifications, each *chelleh* last for forty days) the lover finds in a glimpse.[21]

If the heart of a *salek* wavers between one state and another, it is because he still perceives a duality, for he is still rooted in the attachments of the world. But the heart of a true lover of God is in complete unity and so sees nothing but the Beloved. Love purifies, and all who hope to reach purification must pass through flames of love. But this love is a secret of the heart: to reveal one's love, is to remain corrupted. In that case, when the fire which had entered into the heart has been let loose through the tongue, its flames leave the heart half consumed. A heart thus charred cannot engage itself in the world, the future, or the Beloved; it becomes a useless heart.[22]

Sheikh Ruzbehan Baghli (11th century Sufi) writes in his *Abhar-al-Asheghin* that there are preliminaries for love. It begins in devotion, proceeds into servitude, then to agreement, and then to approval. The reality of love is an affection which is either the product of the blessing of the Beloved or the vision of witnessing the Beloved. The blessing may fall onto the common people, but the vision is reserved for those few who are pure. When love reaches its perfection, it is ecstasy.[23]

Sufis have also divided love into five species:

The highest is Divine love which is the finality of the spiritual journey, and is known only to the truthful.

Another kind of love is intellectual and is proper for the wise; this kind of love is related to the realm of the celestial discovery.

The third type of love is spiritual, and relates to the chosen among human beings, who have stepped out of the realm of animal desire; this kind of love is extremely delicate and tender.

Another species of love is animal attraction which is the limit of the experience of love for those who follow only animal desires, who commit themselves to worthless and selfish habits, and whose wicked actions are the evil fruit of their desires.

And finally, there is also the natural love which all may experience. If such love is guided by the intellect and tempered by spiritual discipline, then it is praiseworthy, but it is valueless if it follows only physical desires.[24]

Sheikh Najmeddin Kubra (12 - 13th century), who was among the greatest Sufis, said that the fire of love disciplines the lover, and the lover confesses in the depths of his being that You are my direction in both the earth and celestial worlds, You are my finality, You are all that is myself.

As Mansur-al-Halaj said,

"I wonder at this 'You' and 'I'.
You have annihilated 'I'.
And there is an 'I' no longer."

Moulana Shah Maghsoud wrote in his book of poetry that,

I was searching for Him in the houses of worship,
As I opened my eyes,
There He was coming to me.
Away from all strangers,
He was coming apparent, He was coming hidden,
Like life itself, hidden and apparent.Who is He?
None but the life of my soul and body.
Neither life nor body would I have without Him.
I am drunken with the eternal Wine.
And the talk of the drunken is not
For many to hear.
I asked, "Who are You?" and He answered me "You."
I asked again, "I?" He replied "No, not you but I!"
With wonderment I understood that He is both within
        and without.
I begged Him to take me away from me,
He said, "You are not other than Me.
There is but one essence whirling within,
Infinity and finite.
Be existence becoming nonexistent,

Drink from this Cup and remain drunk.
Become what you are destined to be, as the
Human is fated to become."[25]

It should be well understood that through the senses can
be gained no understanding of the realm of the Almightiness.
The senses take one into the world of nature, the intellect
brings one to the world of the celestial, and love transports
one to the realm of God. The particular world of the Divine is
the universe of love. All that has been created in that universe
finds its reflection in the mirror of love; all the particles and
the whole of the world are themselves mirrors of the essence
of the realm of Almightiness.[26]

When the *salek* reaches the stage of love, the mirror of
his heart shines pure and clean, and so becomes a mirror of
the whole world. Anything that enters the ocean of Almightiness to reach the shores of Being will be reflected into the
heart of such a *salek*.[27]

Moulana Shah Maghsoud writes, "My salute to the hearts
of those who have sacredly honored the heat of love at the
peak of their youth, those whose hearts remain strong
through their wealth of virtue even when the heat of the sun,
the light of the moon, the heart of the sky, the attraction of
the world, and the ecstasy of life stop."[28] "Rejoicing souls and
clear-sighted eyes love beauty. Their joys do not grow from
repairing the ruins or living in the deep corners of sorrow."[29]

Love is that inner search for the world of beauty, and the
search for beauty has two aspects. One is the search to find
the beauty of qualities, and the other is the longing of the soul
to observe the Beauty of the Essence. The first is common
love illuminated by the light shining onto the world, but the
second is fire, purifying that which exists.[30]

Much the same division of love is expressed in the New
Testament such as reads: "Thou shalt love the Lord thy God
with all thy heart, and with all thy soul, and with all thy
mind", or "Love not the world, neither the things that are in

the world. If any man loves the world, the love of the Father is not in him."

Some believe that Divine trust is Love discovered within the human heart. It reflects itself in the mirror of the heart of a man once he has been cleansed of the dust of impurities so that the face of the Beloved can be seen. Darkness and ignorance are part of human nature, yet the illumination of the heart brings the light of knowledge to us. In one direction, man is bound to the darkness, but in another to the divine living lights. He is truly a complete manifestation, the tension between unity and multiplicity, origin and destiny.[31] Only those who become aware of this duality within themselves, through perceiving the illumination within, can orient themselves toward the light of knowledge.

Majnun was one of the most famous lovers in Persian Sufi poetry; he was in love with Leili, the Beloved. In one of the stories of his love for Leili, someone told him, "Leili is coming." And he replied, "I am Leili. There was a time when seeing her could bring me joy. Now, love is the center of my thought and not her." Majnun at this stage was in the level of burning love, the love which consumes everything in the heart of the lover. Everything vanishes and there remains only love, entire in its purity and radiance.

We read in *Mantegh-al-Teyr* that:

Then the valley of love appears.
And he who enters it falls into flames.
No one may enter but those who deserve such heat,
Those who deserve not this fire are not for this valley.
It is the fire of love,
Love burning hot, love all tumultuous.
Such love as has not a thought for the future.
The lover drowns himself in the fire of hundreds of
    worlds.[32]

Moulana Shah Maghsoud wrote:

I knocked at every door for Wine the night before.
No door opened to me except the door of the heart.
When I entered the heart, I heard:
"Wherever else you stopped was vain,
You should have stopped at the door of heart."[33]

CHAPTER EIGHT

Verd (Zekr, Remembrance)

"Remember Me,
So I shall remember you."
(Koran: II, 152)

Zekr means the remembering of the Divine, as the Almighty Lord command: "Remember Me, so that I remember you," or "Ye who believe, recall God and recall Him often." (Koran: II, 152; XXXIII, 41) Remembering does not mean the occasional recollection of God. Rather it means to remember and remind one's self of His existence at all times. The Prophet Mohammad had called the hearts that remember God the Houses of Heaven.

Worship that is based on traditional customs and empty imitation is bereft of truth, for it is only a fascination of *nafs* and nature and so is separated from reality. It is the heart of the believer that must become open to Being, so that it may see and hear truth until it can believe the reality of the Divine. Without such an understanding and recognition the religion of any man is but a fantasy, since it is a belief in the image of the unknown. The heart must open itself to divine inspiration, and the *zekr* of God prepares the heart for such an opening. Indeed, the Prophet Mohammad advised his followers that the best of deeds is the *zekr* of the Lord. As a *salek* must travel through the successive states of advancement, so the *zekr* that he will be given by the teacher will also have conditions of advancement. The first state of *zekr* that the *zaker* (one who remembers) must accomplish consists in remembering the Divine while putting aside all else; the next level of *zekr* is that the *salek* attempts to remain present in his heart through concentration and meditation;

beyond this, the heart of the believer actually receives the Divine message and is illuminated by the light of his belief.[1]

While perfecting the states of *zekr*, the *salek* also must pass through the stages of *zekr*. Sufis have divided the stages of *zekr* differently, and we only touch upon the basic classifications here: the stages of *zekr* begin with the *zekr* of the tongue, then follows the *zekr* of the heart, and finally the *zekr* of hidden. The *zekr* of the tongue is the verbal *zekr*. It is practiced through the repetition of a phrase or a word as instructed by the Master; the word or the phrase carries the spiritual power of the teacher and so gives energy to the *salek*, aiding him in his concentration. The *zekr* of the heart consists in the constant presence of the *zekr* in the heart. A *salek* reaches this *zekr* through persistence in his verbal *zekr*; when the *zekr* of his tongue and heart become united, he is ready to commence upon his spiritual journey. The *zekr* of the tongue may not at times be as perfect as the *zekr* of the heart, when forgetfulness or fatigue occurs and the *zaker* (performer) forgets his *zekr*. But the *zekr* of the heart is graven with the sign of faith and loyalty, for it consists in remembering the Divine at all times. This remembrance of God, both outwardly and inwardly, is performed in the center of the heart, and as the heart transfers its knowledge to all the body, it purifies the entire human being with its every beat.[2]

To remember God is to remember Him in unity, stripped of the covers and colors of multiplicity. One must necessarily search for that unity within the Divine, and nowhere else. The *zaker* will receive many blessings from the performance of his *zekr*, yet some receive "remember Me, I will remember you;" while others are graciously granted "Call Me, I will answer your prayer." (Koran: II, 152 & XL, 60)[3] The *zekr* that succeeds the *zekr* of heart is the *zekr* of the hidden. This *zekr* is hidden within the heart. It governs and through the heart nourishes the energies of the body. It is through this *zekr* that the *salek* becomes the manifestation of the Divine. Amir-al-Moumenin Ali wrote that the *zekr* becomes intimate with the mind, enlightens the heart, and pours forth blessings onto the *salek*'s life. When such change occurs in the practice of the *zekr*, the *salek* advances to a higher stage of understanding, and this ascension will be comprehensible to the *salek*. He will experience this advancement in such a way that will leave no room for any doubt. In his book *Maghased-ol-Ershad*, Moulana Shah Maghsoud wrote about the *zekr* in the language of poetry:

> *Zekr* is life saturated by the Divine;
> The chest containing the Eternal Names.
> *Zekr* burns down the feather of Gabriel[4]
> Bringing the illumination of love to the heavens of the
>   heart.
> Break the chains that trap your being,
> As you hear the melodies of love inspiring your heart.

To be effective and beneficial, a *zekr* must be given to the *salek* by a teacher; it cannot be read in any book, much less invented by the *salek*. *Zekrs* are given very confidentially only to those students who properly deserve them. One of the *zekrs* that is given to the student is the *zekr* of 'Allah'. Ghosheiri explained that the *zekr* of 'Allah' in the heart frees one from the hands of the enemy and hinders misfortune in entering into the life of the *zaker*.[5] In interpreting his words, it is the conception of the Enemy that is both metaphorical as well as literal. The greatest enemy of the human being on the path of knowledge is ignorance, the state of being of the many. The person who remembers Being and always recollects himself will advance his knowledge on the path of understanding, and in so doing will learn to free himself from the leaden hand of ignorance.

It is narrated from Sheikh Mohammad Shafei Naghshbandi that the *zekr* of heart can be divided into two parts. The sense of the first *zekr* is in the name of Allah and the second is there is no god but Him.

Life is the interaction between the hidden and apparent influences, and the human being is constantly receiving and distributing those energies. Since the rules and laws of harmony and cooperation are among the most effective laws governing the world, the human being receives only those waves for which he has attuned his being to receive. Remembering Divinity attunes the human being with Divinity and allows him to receive what may be called spirituality. These favorable influences are the underlying conditions which help one receive Divine revelation and inspiration. It is narrated from the Prophet that, " Whosoever remembers God, mercy and blessings shall surround him."[6] Zunnun says that whoever remembers God truly and forgets all else at the presence of the Lord, shall have his life filled by His richness.[7] The *zekr* thus involves leaving ignorance behind and stepping forth toward the field of illumination and knowledge.

The *zekr* is the sign of love as one remembers those whom He loves.

Sufis have divided the *zekr* into many stages. In his book *Sala'at*, Moulana Shah Maghsoud, writes about several *zekr*s such as the *zekr* of the tongue, the *zekr* of bodily movements, the *zekr* of the heart, the *zekr* of life, the *zekr* of the hidden, and the *zekr* of the hidden within the hidden. He writes that the highest *zekr* is *"la illaha illa allah"* (There is no god but He, Allah). The perfect *zekr* is the *nama'az* (Muslim prayer), because it is the perfect instruction of unification. The performer of the *zekr* not only repeats this *zekr* verbally, but his physical movements are also part of the same *zekr*. Moulana Shah Maghsoud is the first and the only scholar who has solved the secret hidden in the movements of *nama'az*. The importance of this discovery is that the movements in *nama'az* reveal the great *zekr* of *la illaha illa allah* or as written in the original language:

The successive positions of the *nama'az* are as follows:

ghiam (standing to start the prayer) represents "Alif", |

at the recital of *takbir* the shape is الله

at the time of *ruku* (bowing down) the body posture forms the shape of ﻷ

in *tashahud*, or witnessing, body gesture represents ﻟ

and in *sujud*, or prostration, the body assumes the form of the upside down ﺣﻊ

Together, the physical movements of the performer of the *nama'az* make "*la illaha illa allah*" or لاالهالاالله

Nor does this exhaust the significance of the *zekr* of movements, as Moulana Shah Maghsoud has discovered; other gestures in the *nama'az* also have profound meanings. He writes that there are gestures which also make the shape of

which together is

meaning "He is God." هوالله
Other forms are also revealed such as the reversed which means "alive", الحّی

demonstrating the Koran reading "God is alive and never dies."

The magnificence and the greatness of the *zekr* of *la illaha illa allah* is that its meaning is both verbal, physical, and so also profoundly spiritual: through its performance, the mind, body, and heart are engaged in harmonious remembrance of God. Writing the *zekr* through his physical movements on the page of Being while he utters its words, the *salek* expresses the blessing of oneness.

Such an important discovery by a true Sufi of reality as it truly is cannot pass without notice. As the Koran reads: "This is the book; in it is guidance sure, without doubt, for the pure ones who believe in the unseen are steadfast in prayer, and spend out of what We have provided for them." (Koran: 11, 2-3)

There can be no doubt that the heart of the believer sees the reality hidden from the eyes of the ignorant. The truly wise who discover the rules of existence remain forever inspiring to the deserving few. The knowledge that Sufis speak of is that of Being after complete annihilation of the traveller within it: "All that is on earth will perish, but the Face of thy Lord will abide forever full of Majesty, Bounty, and Honor." (Koran: LV, 26-27)

There have been many debates on why the *nama'az*, following the instructions of the Prophet Mohammad, must be performed through these gestures. Throughout the centuries, no true reason could be found, until Moulana Shah Maghsoud's discovery of this most important secret. What had been a hidden mystery, he has revealed, proving that when the spoken words of God are in the hands of blind imitation, they are hidden behind the curtains of prejudice, fanaticism, and ignorance. Yet despite this, he has shown us through his example that there are thinkers capable of finding the keys that unlock the secrets of reality, and so understanding mysteries where many others failed in their attempts.

If one puts aside any preconceived ideas and looks carefully into the *nama'az*, one will be unable to deny that the goal of Islam is based on the achievement of the absolute perfection of, through, and for Being. Such perfection is revealed in both the manifestation and the sense of worship. All of the wholesome manifestations of knowledge found in the teachings of philosophical theories, in the quest for spirituality, and in the achievement of science, must be considered simply and unabashedly as Divine gifts received through concentration and the purification of the inner self. Such concentration contributes in building a wholesome self who is suffused with honesty, purity, and devotion, both outwardly in his actions and inwardly in his piety.

When the *sala'at* (*nama'az*) is performed by a believer who is aware of both the inner and apparent message, its performance will point towards perfect unification and thus towards divine knowledge. And this reflects the evidence of all of the history of Being, for the perfect human contributes greatly to the advancement of civilization as the realization of truth. He is the individual whose inner knowledge is in perfect harmony with his outward actions.

Here I must caution the reader to put aside whatever preconceptions of Islam that he may have, for Islam is probably the most misunderstood of the world's religions, both in its historic home and also in the West. If one reflects upon the normal state of human affairs, upon the multitude of the ignorant who have difficulty even in separating common sense from the absurdity of their lives, the many prejudices that surround popular conceptions of Islam are not surprising. And quite apart from popular ignorance, Islam has had to contend with the confused and partial understanding of Christianity, and the active obscurantism of Judaism. Is it not almost always the case that any truthful belief ends up in the marketplace of ideas, where it is exhibited to excite the interest of the crowd, and so loses much of its authenticity? For centuries, various heresies have eagerly donned the garments of monotheism, and Islam has been no exception. Heresies and the desires for religious novelties have been encouraged by the traders in religion, whose business is supported by ignorance, prejudice, and fear of knowledge. These traders sometimes, as Moulana Shah Maghsoud said, assume the clothing of friendship, and at other times that of enmity, in order to advertise their poisonous wares under the name of Islam.[8]

From the beginning of human history, the aimless and the greedy have striven to destroy the principles of faith in order to direct the naive towards the destiny of the lost; they have spread their poisonous thoughts throughout human civilization. The path of genuine research and discovery is obscured by thick crusts of dualism and blasphemy, which makes it difficult to discern and even more difficult to follow. Beginners are in particular danger of being misled; in their eagerness to begin the spiritual journey, they may be naive, in their lack of experience they may have difficulty in recognizing false teachers for what they really are. And it is the novice who is the natural prey of those who use religion to cloak their own inner rottenness. Such hypocrites gradually and slowly introduce the signs of their ill intentions into the minds of the naive; and generally these are intentions which grow out of the animal desires, out of the base instincts that humans are born with and can only with difficulty overcome. Having subverted the novice in this way, they can then do with him whatever ignorance and greed permit. The wise can only remark that throughout history, the load of the greedy is always carried on the shoulders of the ignorant—it is their natural burden. [9]

It is recorded from Sheikh Abu Es-hagh Shahriar Kazerouni (10-11th century), that he instructed his followers many times to "Keep the *zekr* of the Almighty Lord in your heart, and keep the world in your hands; and never keep the *zekr* in your tongue and hold the world in your heart." He is reported to have said that it is a misfortune for a cognizant to lose the joy of the *zekr*. As long as one can taste the sweetness of the world, one is deprived from tasting the sweetness of the *zekr*. [10]

Sheihk Najmeddin Kubra, who was one of the greatest Sufis (12th century), wrote in one of his books that *zekr* consists in remembering the Almighty at all times and leaving everything else aside, for one will have to leave behind everything when dead. In this way, it is evident that *zekr* is a mixture of rejection and acceptance. Thus, in the *zekr* of "*la illaha illa allah*" (There is no god except the Almighty), corrupted and impure qualities that foster the spirit of lasciviousness, and act like a teacher to the animal qualities of selfishness, egotism, jealousy, greed, hypocrisy, and sickness of the soul are cast away and negated as one recites "there is no god", in the first part of the *zekr*. That heart which is the House of the Divine and the horizon of the sun of unity is washed from the dust of accidents and the darkness of multiplicity. Believing in the "*la illaha*" (There is no god or idol) brings health to the heart and washes the animal qualities away. The manifestation of the Light of Unity breaks the darkness of multiplicity. Thus, the spirit that is the Caliph of the Divine, ascends to the throne of certitude and witnessing, and so the perfection is made manifest through its radiant beauty. Whatever crude habits and customs that the performer may have are vanquished under the Sun of the Remembered. The dust will perish, and the Beauty of the Remembered will manifest itself in the performer.[11]

CHAPTER NINE

Vafa'a (Loyalty)

Did I not enjoin on you, O, ye children of Adam...?
Koran: XXXVI, 60

Vafa'a signifies loyalty and stability on the path, and fidelity to the principles of the path that one chooses for one's spiritual journey. *Vafa'a* reflects the stability in the heart of the *salek*, and his resulting constancy in progressing toward the direction that he has chosen. *Vafa'a* constitutes a pledge that the *salek* must honor the principles and uphold the disciplines of the path as best he can. If he appears steadfast in times of good fortune, but wavers in times of hardship, he should not be accepted by a truthful teacher of the path of Sufism. The converse is likewise true: the person who desperately reaches toward spirituality when he is distressed or in need, and who is poor in spirit, but who quickly loses his eagerness when the need is met and the pain relieved, demonstrates his lack of loyalty, disgraces himself, and cannot be accepted by teachers of Sufism.

Sufism is not for the weak in character and the poor in spirit, but is a fitting path for the strong who search for knowledge, who are not diverted by good fortune or hardship, who do not stray from the direction that they have freely chosen. By contrast, those who wander and hesitate on the path in their own inner weakness, and so who lose faith with destiny, are like a broken bridge: a bridge that fails may be repaired, but will never be fully trusted.

Sufi teachers give general instructions and let their students learn the disciplines of the path, but special instructions are always kept in reserve for those who are exceptional, those who are eager to learn and firm in their victory over the temptations of their animal desires. Only those who are steadfast can be worthy of trust in the school of Sufism, and they are those who remain virtuous, disciplined, and strong in their faith.

Hafez says:

I endure all hardship
Remain loyal and joyful in my faith.
Discontentment is infidelity in my religion.

CHAPTER TEN

Fard (Isolation)

I searched for freedom, I found it in solitude.
I searched for serenity, I found it in silence.
Sheikh Abul Hassan Kharaghani (10th century)

Fard represents withdrawal from the world into the purity of isolation, solitude, and the process of becoming. The great Sufis of the first century after the advent of Islam all taught that health and spiritual serenity is best achieved through isolation from the crowd and all its base desires and shallow thinking. This is because the heart that remains within the bondage of materialistic desires is entrapped there, and thus sickly; the desires of the world so permeate every facet of worldly society as to endanger the health of the heart of one who lives continually amidst them. Such an illness is enough to destroy the nascent purity of the heart,to plunge it back into the corruption of the multitude, and certainly to prevent the cleansing process of purification that is essential to spiritual growth. Therefore, since to become free from the diseases of the *nafs* is to recover the health of the heart, such health may be achieved only when the human being isolates himself from the vulgar world of the many, and sets himself free from the desires of the crowd that it embodies.

The stage of *fard* is achieved when the Sufi passes beyond the uncertain stages of happenstance and accident. Little by little, through practice, meditation, and thorough study, the *salek* begins to feel himself set apart from the multitude; he begins to perceive his own self, his own heart, and through this process of dawning understanding instinctively yearns for separation from pollution, and so strives to set himself apart. If he is a knowledgeable and reasonable person he will also intellectually recognize that he can set himself free from the occurrence of accidents and the bondage of the limitations which they impose. But solitude does not imply sitting in the corner of a dark room away from society, which would be but a negative type of isolation; rather, it consists in finding the way toward understanding that is hindered by the covers of misunderstandings, gossip, lack of knowledge, and secondhand information that is not the proper knowledge of a *salek*. To be sure, the *salek* will remove himself from the society of the vulgar; his manners and tastes will become more refined and more intellectual, but this does not imply a renunciation of human society, but rather its purification. Although this is largely an inward direction, nevertheless it has outward manifestations that the *salek*'s friends and acquaintances will notice. He will become more dignified in his bearing, less ready to offer hasty opinions—in a word, more thoughtful. He will certainly take more effort in his study, in a sense which he could not previously have understood. Here, in the *salek*'s proper yearning for knowledge and its purity, he should be careful not to attempt too much too soon. The danger lies in the fact that the *salek* may mistake mere information or secondhand knowledge for his own authentic knowledge in his eagerness to understand, and so remain in the bondage of ideas that he has no real understanding of.

Understanding and research on the meaning of abstractions through acquired information is not an acceptable method for a Sufi. One does not become a Sufi, or advance along the path, by merely reading what others have discovered. Instead, Sufis instruct their students to set themselves free from the imprisonment of acquired and borrowed information since this kind of superficial knowledge will not help the *salek* on the path of his inner journey. Acquired knowledge is the greatest veil between the human being and the reality within, because its truth, though real, is not actually experienced. This is a danger precisely because, for most people, even secondhand knowledge is a rare commodity: and to be knowledgeable even through the efforts of others is more than most are capable of. Prophet Mohammad says that, "knowledge is not in the skies that pour on you, it does not grow from the soil like a plant, but it is hidden within you: qualify yourself for the divine quality, until you discover it."

For those who are not familiar with the spiritual journey, it may seem difficult to step beyond the information of the senses and give such knowledge no place among the bases for the spiritual journey. But we must understand that the senses are not the most important avenues of understanding, and realize that compared to the reality within, the senses are of a limited and small power, an insignificant part of the magnificent power hidden within the human being. If we reflect upon the many mistakes that the senses make, we can begin to see how their power is limited and thus unable to provide the most accurate knowledge that the spiritual journey demands. Knowledge gained from the senses is like information learned through rumor: attractive as it may be, it is secondhand.

The rules of spirituality cannot be understood unless they are experienced. The logic of our senses consists in understanding nature by encountering it; we cannot expect the senses to direct us to the spiritual path or to guide us along our way. It is narrated from the Prophet in the *Sacred Hadith* that "whatever you distinguish and create by your own imagination, even if it has the closest approximation to reality, is still your imagination and has no ground for in reality." The importance of the stage of *fard* lies in separating oneself from the illusions that surround one. After accomplishing the stage of *fard*, the *salek* will become more stable and steadfast on his quest. He learns to distinguish truth from error, and so such obstacles will not prevent him from arriving at the destination he has chosen to achieve. There is one important note that I must emphasize for the reader, and that is when the *salek* learns to separate himself from the effects of society and his surroundings, it does not mean that he may become care-less in following those rules which hold the society together. Simply by cleansing himself from association with the vulgar multitude does not give him a license to ignore the rules of civil society. On the contrary, the concentration of the thoughts and spiritual meditation make the individual a better member of society, even though the innate value of most of its members be slight. The *salek* becomes an individual who will contribute to his society through his knowledge and pre-vent others from following the roads to destruction; indeed, he cannot help but contribute to the common welfare as he has the rare gift of knowledge, and so can distinguish truth from error.

Fard, then, is a freedom from the accidents of this world and from the preoccupation with the future. It may also be regarded as a fundamental separation from everything but God. The Sufi is absorbed and attracted only by the Provider of all things: he is neither possessed nor has he any posses-sions. The Sufi is a single abstract individual. The term "single abstract" in the language of Sufism refers to the union of the apparent and the inward solitude. Apparent solitude is achieved when the Sufi possesses nothing from this world, while inward solitude expresses the Sufi's freedom from the preoccupation with the future. He asks for nothing except God. He empties his mind and heart of all else. He is the seeker of reality, and reality alone is what he searches for.

Desires and their attachments are but covers of the real-ity of life. Desire is a burden on the shoulders of a *salek*, a burden which he seeks to lighten and so more quickly reach the peaceful and successful result of his journey. The Prophet Mohammad referred to the world as the place of calamity, and to the extent that calamity is reduced, so much the better for the seeker of reality.[1] He ordered mankind to lighten their burden, since heavy loads are hard to carry. The distractions of the mind and the desires for things are merely veils hiding the inner richness and wealth. When a *salek* becomes a singularity apart from all the multiplicity that surrounds him, he will grow closer to the stage of unity. [2]

The process of achieving simplicity can be understood as the abstraction of the *salek* from the world. Abstraction signifies the turning away from the occupations of the world and the intrusions of the desires. It is the freedom of the mind, the settlement of nature into solitude. The *salek* abstracts himself from the distractions of the world as he pulls away from them; from his distance he sees that they are but veils that cover reality: a wise man does not join but leaves the enemy far away.[3]

A *salek* must walk onto the path of abstraction as Jesus did. Jesus owned nothing from this world except a comb and a cup. Once, he saw a poor man trying to comb his hair with his fingers and drink water from the palm of his hand. Then and there, Jesus threw the comb and cup away. He lived the life of an single abstract individual.[4] It is this kind of abstraction that is enriched by spiritual wealth.

The most abstracted ones among the followers of the Prophet Mohammad were the People of Suffe. They had nothing from this world. The Prophet instructed them to add *Tafrid*, or isolation, to their abstraction, since those who are the most isolated can better walk on the path of reality.[5]

The great Sufi Hazrat Mir Ghotbeddin Mohammad wrote in his *Eshragh Nameh* [6] that isolation and solitude guard one from unnecessary relationships, and absolve one from the lowly crowd. Unnecessary relationships, especially with the unworthy, distract one's mind, leading it away from the straight path into desire, while being part of a crowd may well result in being influenced by the morality of the masses, which is not a recipe for a good or even a safe result.

Among the saying of Ba Yazid is that, "I have taken different steps toward the Almighty Lord. But the only step which could take me to the House of solitude was the step of the heart." "After forty years of mortification, one night the curtain dropped, and I begged: 'Please, let me into the House

of Your Presence.' I heard: 'You own a cup and a robe, you
may not be permitted entrance.' I dropped the cup and the
robe, and so the revelation came to me." What Ba Yazid is
teaching us here by relating his experience is that even after
forty years of striving and mortification, he was not granted
what he sought until he dropped his cup and robe and so
released himself from all low attachments. By contrast, how
then could the pretenders of religious piety and claimants of
purity who are so extremely attracted to the world, even
imagine that they might be permitted to approach the House
of closeness?[7] Ba Yazid has also been recorded as saying that
"When I reached the stage of closeness, I received an inspiration telling me to ask for what I wished. I said that I did not
have any wish, I would rather You ask something for me.
Again I received an inspiration telling me: 'Ask from Me.' I
said: 'All I want is You.' I heard my reply and He said: 'As
long as there is even a bit remaining from Ba Yazid, such a
wish cannot be granted.' Thus I understood that there should
remain no 'I' to ask for any wish."[8]

CHAPTER ELEVEN

Faghr (Poverty)

My poverty is my honor.
Prophet Mohammad

In the Arabic language *faghr* means the condition of poverty, while a *faghir* (sometimes spelled *faqir*) is one who is poor. In the language of Sufism, *faghir* refers to the Sufi or *darvish*: since the Sufi is free from all attachments to material goods, and also free from the influences of the desires, he is therefore poor, possessing nothing and letting nothing possess himself. It has been narrated of the Prophet that " My poverty is my honor." The Prophet's honor has a dual aspect: poverty in terms of the absence of possessions, but honor that flows from placing the graciousness of God so far above the material world that any of its goods are of no account. Hazrat Jallaleddin Ali, one of the great Sufis of the nineteenth century, wrote that "The goal of a Sufi is not to become a beggar, but to free himself from the attractions of the world. One can be a Sufi even with a royal crown on one's brow." And indeed, such was the case for the Safavi Kings who ruled over Iran centuries ago, many of whom were Sufis.

There is a story told of Nur Ali Shah, one of the most influential Sufis in history. It is said that Nur Ali Shah was dwelling in the desert in a tent, with his followers living about him in their tents. Nur Ali Shah's tent was the most beautiful and the most expensive tent ever made, woven of threads of silver, gold, and silk, and held to the ground with golden spikes. A man who heard about this great Sufi teacher came to the desert in hope of serving him and learning from his teachings. Admitted to the presence of the Sufi master, he sat a while until Nur Ali Shah said to his visitor, "Let us walk." So they began to walk, farther and farther away the tent village. Finally the man became tired and asked the Sufi, "When would you return to your tent?" Nur Ali Shah replied, "I will never turn from the direction in which I am going." The man said, "Then what will happen to the tent and all those golden tent-spikes?" He replied, "Those golden spikes were not driven into my heart but only into the heart of the ground."

Faghr has been given three signs. It has been likened to the brightness of the sun as its first sign: it shines upon everything and everyone and does not withhold its reflection from anything. The second sign of *faghr* is the humility that is likened to the humility of the earth, which endures everyone, both good or wicked, who treads upon it; earth does not change its position because of the goodness or badness of those who dwell on it. The third sign is generosity, likened to that of the clouds. The clouds scatter their rain over everything, over ocean and desert, garden and graveyard; clouds give with generosity whether such generosity is understood or not.[1]

The essence of the achievement of *faghr* lies in the silence of the *nafs*, the life of the heart, and the silence of the tongue. The difference between a *faghir* and a beggar is that the world has abandoned the beggar, yet a *faghir* has abandoned the world.[2]

A *salek* abandons four aspects of the world in becoming a *faghir:* He abandons material wealth, the ambition for position, the indulgence of desire, and finally his ego.[3]

There are ten principles for the *salek* to accomplish which may be understood as requirements to fulfill in attaining *faghr:*

1. A *zekr* instructed by a Master,
2. Meditation
3. Isolation from the multitude
4. Leaving the attachments of the world, both present and future,

5. Knowledge of the rules of the path,
6. Acting according to what one has learned,
7. Sincerity, so that whatever is done, is done for God.
8. Satisfaction in whatever is received from God.
9. Annihilation, severing one's "self" from all the desires and worthless qualities,
10. The way of being, that is annihilation of one's characteristics and qualities, while remaining alive solely within the essence of the Divine.

And there are ten illuminations that accompany these principles. These stages of illuminations are:

Confession; Honesty; Obedience; Thankfulness; Patience; Trustworthiness; Kindness; Mortification; Cognition; Certainty. The path to *faghr* is the path of necessity, charted by the demands of truthfulness, honesty, and belief which accompany the Sufi on his journey. The origin of *faghr* is the love that has its essence in knowing the Divine. The fruit of the *faghr* is understanding, its wealth of contentment.[4]

Gosheiri writes that poverty is the watchword of the saints, the ornament of the pious, and the will of the Divine for His chosen ones. A *faghir* is the chosen among the people, because he is the treasure chest of the Divine secret.[5]

The tablet of a man's heart will be made pure of the contamination of the material world and its attractions through acts of purification and meditation. The essence of the human being grows pure through the heat of love. What remains of the seeker after such striving toward purification is a heart entirely pure and thus illuminated. This is the heart that has been referred to as the mirror reflecting God. One who has been purified in this way is called a *faghir*, whose chest is the holy place for the manifestation of divine illumination, whose very being is like the great elixir. To accompany such a perfect being is the equivalent of serving the Almighty directly.

Sufis have said that the *Murshed* (Master) is like a mirror in which the *salek* sees his own being reflected back, perceiving himself truly as he could not do unaided; thus, he strives to correct and discipline himself according to the instructions of the Master. As the *salek* passes the different stages of self-understanding, he gradually grows more and more aware of his own being, which is why the way of Sufism is truly the path of self-cognition.

Prophet Mohammad said that the key to paradise is to accompany a *faghir*, since *fughara* (plural of *faghir*) are the companions of God. Aziz Nassafi, one of the great Sufis, wrote that God will not let a nation perish unless that nation despises its *fughara*. Yahya Ibn Maaz said that a *faghir* is attracted only toward God, since he has no reason to depend on anything other than God.[6]

A *salek* must perfect four qualities in order to become a *faghir*. He must have knowledge to keep himself inwardly stable and constant; he must attain piety to keep himself away from distractions; he must achieve certainty to help him keep to the path, and have a *zekr* to accompany him at all times.[7] Beyond these necessary prerequisites, Ibn Khafif said that to be a *darvish* is to abandon properties and step out of qualities, while Messri emphasizes the more general freedom from attachments, saying that the *darvish* does not have any property and is not the property of anyone.[8]

There is a story narrated by the Sufi scholar Katani. He said that, "Once in Mecca I saw a young man dressed in tattered clothes who always kept his silence. I told myself that I should give some money to this man, since he seemed to be so poor, so I put 200 silver coins on his prayer rug, hoping that he would accept it as a gift. As I put the money on the rug, he looked at me deeply and said, 'I have chosen closeness to God over seventy thousand coins, and now you want to tempt me with these?' He threw the silver away and left, leaving me to gather up the scattered coins. I had never seen glory like that of his and I have never felt more ashamed: I saw that since he was the strength that spurned wealth and cast it aside, while I was the weakness who was gathering up what he had thrown away."[9]

The *salek* of the path of the truth will not arrive at the stage of *faghr* unless through asceticism and piety. As long as the desires for the world remain in the mind, *faghr* will not find its way to the heart.

Fughara are of several types. There are those who do not see themselves possessing anything from the world, even though they may technically have legal possessions. These individuals give of their wealth without expecting anything in return. Next are those who do not see even their worshipping or prayers as their possessions; and so they pray out of love of the Divine without expecting any reward. Yet another group of *fughara* do not see anything relating to the world, to worship, or even to their own grace and generosity as forming their belongings. They see only the grace and blessing of the Lord.

The next group are those who do not relate their essence and existence to any feeling of belonging and possessing. Indeed, they do not even see the origin of their selves as belonging to them in any way. Their position is described as: "*faghir* needs nothing." This is why Prophet Mohammad says, "My *faghr* is my honor." This is the highest position for a *faghir* to attain and this category of Sufis is higher than the common people can understand or know: they are known only to God. God conceals these few from the eyes of the multitude. This rank of *faghr* is the rank of Sufi masters, not that of the *salek*, student, and follower.[10] Moulana Shah Maghsoud says that the knowledge of *faghr* demands the abandonment of possessions, the limitations of thought, and all narrow-mindedness. *Faghr* is achieved through the united powers of the self, the soul, the mind, and the heart, since the principle of *darvishi* is the elevation of the heart toward the Almighty God without any medium and cover.[11]

Faghr is the confession of poverty; and that depends on stepping out of the limited self and patiently striving toward the Divine path. Its faith is reliance on God and its achievement is unification with Him. The keys to *faghr* are striving, searching, and devotion. *Faghr* is the Divine treasure and its

place is the house of the heart. The wellspring of *faghr* is love
and its reality is achieved through annihilation.[12]

Sufism is a hidden treasure, not goods that can be
bought or sold in the marketplace. The Sufis have released
themselves from the world of mortality, they have passed the
stages of purification, have freed themselves from attachment
to the realm of appearance, and have striven for the annihilation of their limited "self" into the eternal Being.

CHAPTER TWELVE

Fana (Annihilation)

*"Oh Dear Lord, how much longer must there be an 'I' and
a 'You' between us?
Take away this ego from me, so that there remains nothing
of me, but all of You."*
Ba Yazid Bastami

"All will perish: except the Face of thy Lord will abide
forever." (Koran: LV, 26, 27) *Fana* means annihilation and in
the language of Sufism it refers to several related concepts.
First there is the annihilation of the spiritual traveller into
God, in which human qualities are annihilated into the qualities of the Divine. The human being, in his limitation as part
of creation, carries perishable qualities and many faults; but
also he is the essence of Being in his limitlessness, and therefore can approach and master the Divine qualities. The goal
of a Sufi is to move always closer to the understanding of the
reality of God, which means the careful recognition of divine
qualities within the self and the purging of contingent earthly
qualities.

Fana is a stage which a Sufi reaches after he has perfected his inner purification, concentration, meditation, and
prayer to the point of being able to discover the inner sense
and the reality of Being. Even though a *salek* will have the
experience of spirituality during his journey towards God, the
continual and all-knowing discovery of spirituality comes after arriving at the stage of annihilation. At the stage of *fana*,
the imaginary walls of the limited self will fall, and the *salek*
enters the *seyr* in God (*Seyr fe Allah*). At this stage, he will
directly witness the stable and absolute essence (*ayane
sabetheh*) of the eternal existence and so will discover the

meaning of Divinity. The Koran proclaims that all will perish except the face of thy Lord. In other words, all the limited manifestations of the created world will dissolve, and what remains will be the essence of reality which is the Divine.

Every changing manifestation of existence has its basis in that stable and unchangeable essence which is eternal. To know the face of the Creator is that knowledge for which the Sufi strives. Moulana Shah Maghsoud explained that knowledge is the annihilation of the knower into the known, or the union of the knower and the known into the awareness of knowledge. The Sufi is that individual who finds the gem of the knowledge in the depth of his being, and seeks to know it through annihilation into it. At the stage of *fana*, the *salek* will arrive at the reality of the truth of Being, for it is at this stage that the *salek* becomes a Sufi: he now has the direct experience of religion, where religion is reality the universal path for those who long to know reality as reality is.

Let us examine the meaning of the word "annihilation". Annihilation is losing the limited self into the being of existence and breaking out of physical dimensions that define the world of limitation and possibility. It may appear to be a mystical term explaining the unattainable. However, if one looks carefully with the eye of insight, one will see that 'annihilation' is but the unavoidable process of being. Even though through the eyes of matter, there is an apparent boundary around every object, living or inanimate, a boundary that reflects the capacities and uses of the senses, there is no real separation between any particle of the existence. Every element of being is connected and bound to every other element, so gracefully and with such great skill, that nothing can separate existence into truly discrete parts, even if Being itself should desire it. Thus, the whole of existence is but the one and only existing Being.

To learn and understand the wholeness of existence one must break the boundary and truly find one's own essential existence after being annihilated into that abstractness of being. In other words, to know the rule, one must become the rule. Since Being is for mankind, nothing that can exist is beyond the reach of a human being. Sufism seeks the logic of Being to attain this reach of understanding.

The reality of Being may not be understood unless one experiences the Unification. It is said that the human being is the smaller world capable of understanding the greater universe. He is not separated from that greater universe, the visible unrealistic boundaries of which make him see himself as separate, different, and an isolated being. Existing within and believing in this limitation is called ignorance in Sufism. The *salek* must step out of the realm of ignorance and into the realm of knowledge.

Annihilation can open the door toward discovering the secrets of God. As long as the bubble floats upon the ocean, it is separated from the ocean because of the emptiness inside it; it is also separated from the knowledge of the ocean, its qualities and its power. Whatever it may see and pretend to understand is only illusion, for as soon as it loses its boundary and is annihilated into the ocean, it is no longer a bubble or a drop of water: it becomes the ocean and inseparable from it.

It is narrated from Ba Yazid that "The first time I went on a pilgrimage to Mecca, I saw the House; the second time I saw the Owner of the House; the third time I saw neither the House nor the Owner, for I was annihilated into the Divine."[1] Once someone wished to meet Ba Yazid, and went to Ba Yazid's house and knocked at the door. Opening the gate, Ba Yazid asked the man what it was he wanted, to which the man replied that he would like to see Ba Yazid. Ba Yazid answered him: "Poor Ba Yazid! I have been searching for him for the last thirty years, but have found no sign of him." Therefore, as long as there is an 'I' who worships God, there remains a final veil between the 'I' and the Divine. The 'I' must dissolve in order for the veil to be lifted and the Divine recognized and known.

Rumi says:
No one is admitted to the palace of the Lord
Unless he is annihilated.
Ascension is becoming nonexistent
It is nonexistence that is the stage for lovers.
It is time to become completely poor
To leave the *nafs* and become all of life.

The logic behind the stage and the practice of annihilation can be understood only through the spiritual knowledge that a Sufi attains.

As the stage before existence, annihilation involves erasing all that remains of the worthless excess of existence, emptying oneself so that one remains only through Divinity. In actuality, annihilation is not a synonym for "not being" rather it refers to "being". The *salek* is to die from the world of limitation (that S/he must in any event leave forever someday), and live for the command of Divine love. This death does not refer to the actual death of the body, as the one who has not learned the art of "becoming" will never live whether he is physically dead or alive. Rather it refers to freeing one's self from the boundary of limitation. When the traveller is annihilated completely, he will rise and exist in the Divine.[2] ("Whoever works righteousness and has Faith, verily, to him will We give a new life, a life that is good and pure..." (Koran: XVI, 97)

Attar writes that those who are free from their ego become united with God at the stage of selflessness. They leave the transient 'self' behind, and will exist through the existence of the Friend. They are the gem within the shell, not the shell.

Two levels of annihilation may be distinguished: outward annihilation and inner annihilation. Outward annihilation is the annihilation of all actions into the Divine will. This level is reached when the *salek* completely frees himself from low human motivations and qualities, and ascends to those of Divinity. At this stage, the *salek* sees the manifestation of the Divine in everything.

Beyond this stage, inner annihilation is the annihilation of all qualities within those of Divinity. That is when the *salek* is dissolved into the divine existence and breaks the limitation of the self. Until the *salek* has passed this stage of annihilation, he is not truly a monotheist since his notion of God is still based in his imagination. As long as there is 'I' and 'You', and so a worshipper and worshipped existing apart, the traveller is still a dualist not a monotheist. Those who pass the stage of annihilation and exist after this stage may alone truly be considered to be practicing, understanding monotheists. The one who truly believes in unity is the one who has been annihilated into the single essence through his understanding, and has broken forth from the limits of the self and the bonds of physical existence to become one with a universe beyond the limitations of nature.

References

Non-English quotations are the author's own translations.
Many of the following books are written by ancient Sufis and philosophers edited and compiled by researchers and printed in the specified places and dates.

Introduction

1. John Alden Williams, ed., *Islam*, New York: George Braziller, 1961, p. 137.
2. Ali Kianfar, Ph. D., *Oveyse Gharan and the History of His School*, California: Yuin University Publication, 1983, p. 16.
3. Ali Kianfar, Ph. D., p. 17.
4. Ali Kianfar, Ph. D., p. 17.
5. Many Sufis have written longative treatises on the shortcomings of the philosophy as the tool to achieve a truthful understanding regarding the secrets of the existence. For example, Sheikh Shahabeddin Suhrevardi who is one of the outstanding figures in Sufism has written extensively to oppose philosophy as the key to human understanding.
6. Ali Kianfar, Ph. D., p.18.
7. Mir Abul Fazl Angha, *Anvar-e-Ghulub Salekin*, Teheran: 1359/ 1980, p. 23.
8. *Chelleh* is forty days of practice under the guidance of the spiritual teacher.

Chapter One

1. Seyyed Jafar Sajadi, *Farhang-e-Lughat va Estalahat Erfani*, Teheran: 1354 (1975), p. 469.
2. Abul Ghasem Ghosheiri, *Resaleh Ghosheiri*, edited and translated into Farsi by Badiezaman Furozanfar, Teheran: 1346, p. 226.
3. Abul Ghasem Ghosheiri, p. 230.
4. Ghotbeddin Abul Muzaffar Ebadi, *Sufi Nameh*, Teheran: 1347, p. 227.
5. Parables and metaphors are all for learning and advancing one's

self to the level of truthful understanding. The story of Adam, his descension and the temptation motivated by the Devil is the story related to all who step down from the essence of being, tempted by the change of the short living waves of life and ultimately deprived from the tanquility of heaven and fall into the change of hell guided by distractions of the unknown.

6. Ghotbeddin Abul Muzaffar Ebadi, p. 227.

7. Ezeddin Mohammad Kashani, *Mesbahul Hedaye va Meftahol Kefaeh*, Teheran: 1325, p. 345.

8. Ezeddin Mohammad Kashani, p. 345.

9. Abul Ghasem Ghosheiri, p. 216.

10. Ghotbeddin Abul Muzaffar Ebadi, p. 226.

11. Abul Ghasem Ghosheiri, p. 231.

12. Ghotbeddin Abul Muzaffar Ebadi, pp. 119-120.

13. Moulana Shah Maghsoud, *A Meditation: Payam-e-Del*, trans. Nahid Angha, 1992, p. 13.

14. Abul Ghasem Ghosheiri, p. 217.

15. Abul Ghasem Ghosheiri, p. 217.

16. Ezeddin Mohammad Kashani, p. 325.

17. Abul Ghasem Ghosheiri, p. 241.

18. Sheikh Shahubeddin Suhrevardi, *Awaref-al Maaref*, Cairo, 1939, p.162.

19. Sheikh Shahubeddin Suhrevardi, p. 162.

Chapter Two

1. Seyyed Jafar Sajadi, *Farhang-e-Lughat va Estalahat Erfani*, Teheran: 1354 (1975), p. 469.

2. Sheikh Ahmad Ja'am, *Onso Tabein va Seratolah Mubin*, Teheran: 1350, p. 68.

3. Sheikh Ahmad Ja'am, p. 69.

4. Moulana Shah Maghsoud, *Serajol Huda*, Teheran: 1978, p. 28.

5. Abul Ghasem Ghosheiri, *Resaleh Ghosheiri*, edited and translated by Badiezaman Furozanfar, Teheran: 1346, p. 145.

6. Ghotbeddin Abul Muzaffar Ebadi, *Sufi Nameh*.

7. Sheikh Ahmad Ja'am, p. 74.

8. Moulana Shah Maghsoud, *Serajol Huda*, p. 28.

Chapter Three

1. Ghotbeddin Abul Muzaffar Ebadi, *Sufi Nameh*, Teheran: 1347, p. 59.

2. Ghotbeddin Abul Muzaffar Ebadi, p. 59.
3. Ghotbeddin Abul Muzaffar Ebadi, p. 60.
4. Ghotbeddin Abul Muzaffar Ebadi, p. 61.
5. Abul Ghasem Ghosheiri, *Resaleh Ghosheiri*, edited and translated into Farsi by Badiezaman Furozanfar, Teheran: 1346, p. 39.
6. Abul Ghasem Ghosheiri, p. 167.
7. Ghotbeddin Abul Muzaffar Ebadi, p. 92.
8. Ghotbeddin Abul Muzaffar Ebadi, p. 93.
9. Ghotbeddin Abul Muzaffar Ebadi, p. 94.
10. Ghotbeddin Abul Muzaffar Ebadi, p. 97.
11. Abul Ghasem Ghosheiri, p. 162.

Chapter Four

1. Abul Ghasem Ghosheiri, *Resaleh Ghosheiri*, edited and translated into Farsi by Badiezaman Furozanfar, Teheran: 1346, p. 280.
2. Abul Ghasem Ghosheiri, p. 287.
3. Ghotbeddin Abul Muzaffar Ebadi, *Sufi Nameh*, Teheran: 1347, p. 72.
4. Abul Ghasem Ghosheiri, p. 284.
5. Ghotbeddin Abul Muzaffar Ebadi, p. 71.
6. Ghotbeddin Abul Muzaffar Ebadi, p. 73.
7. Ghotbeddin Abul Muzaffar Ebadi, pp. 75-76.
8. Ezeddin Mohammad Kashani, *Mesbahul Hedaye va Meftahol Kefaeh*, Teheran: 1325, p. 370.
9. Ezeddin Mohammad Kashani, pp. 380-381.
10. Abul Ghasem Ghosheiri, p. 297.
11. Abul Ghasem Ghosheiri, p. 298.
12. Jelleleddin Mohammad Molavi, Rumi, *Masnavi*.
13. Hazrat Mir Ghotbeddin Mohammad Angha, *Destination: Eternity*, trans. Nahid Angha, California: International Association of Sufism.

Chapter Five

1. Ezeddin Mohammad Kashani, *Mesbahul Hedaye va Meftahol Kefaeh*, Teheran: 1325 p. 341.
2. Abul Ghasem Ghosheiri, *Resaleh Ghosheiri*, p. 328.
3. Abul Ghasem Ghosheiri, p. 330.
4. Abul Ghasem Ghosheiri, p. 331.
5. Ghotbeddin Abul Muzaffar Ebadi, *Sufi Nameh*, p. 118.
6. Ghotbeddin Abul Muzaffar Ebadi, p. 119.

7. Ghotbeddin Abul Muzaffar Ebadi, p. 120.
8. Ghotbeddin Abul Muzaffar Ebadi, p. 401.
9. Sheikh Ahmad Ja'am, *Rosat-al Maznabin*, Teheran: 1355, p.156.
10. Sheikh Ahmad Ja'am, p. 156.
11. Sheikh Ahmad Ja'am, p. 158.
12. Moulana Shah Maghsoud, *Payam-e-Del*, p. 17.
13. From Khajeh Mohammad Hafez, *Divan*, Teheran: 1320.
14. Moulana Shah Maghsoud, p. 10.
15. Moulana Shah Maghsoud p. 10.
16. Moulana Shah Maghsoud p. 12.
17. Ghotbeddin Abul Muzaffar Ebadi, p. 49.

Chapter Six
1. Seyyed Jafar Sajadi, *Farhang-e-Lughat va Estalahat Erfani*, Teheran: 1354 (1975), p. 305.
2. Seyyed Jafar Sajadi, *Farhang-e-Lughat va Estalahat Erfani*, Teheran: 1354 (1975), p. 310.
3. Seyyed Jafar Sajadi, *Farhang-e-Lughat va Estalahat Erfani*, Teheran: 1354 (1975), p. 310.
4. Abul Ghasem Ghosheiri, *Resaleh Ghosheiri*, edited and trans. by Badiuzaman Fruzanfar, Teheran: 1982, p. 322.
5. Abul Ghasem Ghosheiri, p. 333.
6. Abul Ghasem Ghosheiri, p. 325.
7. Sheikh Ahmad Ja'am, *Onso-Tabein*, p. 82.
8. Moulana Shah Maghsoud narrated from one of his lectures.
9. Sheikh Ahmad Ja'am, p. 84.
10. Sheikh Ahmad Ja'am, p. 87.
11. Ghotbeddin Abul Muzaffar Ebadi, *Sufi Nameh*, p. 100.
12. Ghotbeddin Abul Muzaffar Ebadi, p. 101.
13. Ghotbeddin Abul Muzaffar Ebadi, p. 101.
14. Jellaleddin Mohammad Molavi, Rumi, *Masnavi*.
15. Sheikh Ahmad Ja'am, *Rozat-maznabin*, p. 205.
16. Moulana Shah Maghsoud, *Nirvan*, trans. Nahid Angha, California: 1992. (under print.)

Chapter Seven
1. From Moulana Shah Maghsoud, *Divan-e-Ghazal*, book of Poetry.
2. Khajeh Mohammad Hafez, *Divan*, p. 192.
3. Moulana Shah Maghsoud, *Maghased-al-Ershad*, Teheran: 1359, p. 14.

4. Sheikh Farideddin Attar Neyshapouri, *Mantegh al Tayr*, Teheran: 1341 (1962), pp. 222-223.
5. Ghazi Abu Bakr Hamideddin Balkhi, *Maghamat Hamidi*, Teheran: 1312, p. 129.
6. Sheikh Ahmad Ja'am, *Rozat-ol-Maznabein*, p. 124.
7. Sheikh Ahmad Ja'am, p. 127.
8. Sheikh Najmeddin Razi, *Eshgh va Aghl*, Teheran: 1345, p. 62.
9. Sheikh Najmeddin Razi, p. 63.
10. Sheikh Ahmad Ja'am, p. 129.
11. Sheikh Ahmad Ja'am, p. 133.
12. Abul Ghasem Ghosheiri, *Resaleh Ghosheiri*, p. 552.
13. Abul Ghasem Ghosheiri, p. 562.
14. Abul Ghasem Ghosheiri, p. 565.
15. Abul Ghasem Ghosheiri, p. 570.
16. Sheikh Najmeddin Razi, *Eshgh va Aghl*, p. 58.
17. Sheikh Najmeddin Razi, p. 62.
18. Sheikh Najmeddin Razi, p. 65.
19. Ezeddin Nassafi, *Insan-e- Ka'amel*, Teheran: 1341, p. 113.
20. Ezeddin Nassafi, p. 114.
21. Ezeddin Nassafi, p. 115.
22. Ezeddin Nassafi, p. 188.
23. Bagheri, *Aghtab-e-Oveysi*, Teheran: 1353, III, p. 109.
24. Bagheri, *Aghtab-e-Oveysi*, Teheran: 1353, p. 110.
25. Moulana Shah Maghsoud, *Divan*, p. 112.
26. Ezeddin Nassafi, p. 172.
27. Ezeddin Nassafi, p. 173.
28. Moulana Shah Maghsoud, *A Meditation: Payam-e Del*, trans. Nahid Angha, under print.
29. Moulana Shah Maghsoud, *A Meditation: Payam-e-Del*
30. Ezeddin Mohammad Kashani, *Mesbahul Hedaye va Meftahol Kefaeh*, p. 404.
31. Moulana Shah Maghsoud, p. 7
32. Sheikh Fakhreddin Attar, *Manteg al Teyr*, pp. 222-223.
33. Nahid Angha, *Selections*, California, 1991.

Chapter Eight

1. Ezeddin Mohammad Kashani, *Maghased-ol-Ershad*, pp. 20-21.
2. Ghotbeddin Abul Muzaffar Ebadi, *Sufi Nameh*, p. 79.
3. Ghotbeddin Abul Muzaffar Ebadi, p. 80.
4. In the language of Sufism, Gabriel is the intellect.

5. Abul Ghasem Ghosheiri, *Resaleh Ghosheiri*, p. 348.
6. Ghotbeddin Abul Muzaffar Ebadi, p. 27.
7. Abul Ghasem Ghosheiri, p. 348.
8. Moulana Shah Maghsoud, *Sala'at*, Teheran: 1978, p. 115.
9. Moulana Shah Maghsoud, p. 115-116.
10. Bagheri, *Aghtab-e-Oveysi*, Teheran:1353, II, p. 250.
11. Bagheri, III, p. 238.

Chapter Ten

1. Ghotbeddin Abul Muzaffar Ebadi, *Sufi Nameh*, p. 128.
2. Ghotbeddin Abul Muzaffar Ebadi, p. 129.
3. Ghotbeddin Abul Muzaffar Ebadi, p. 129.
4. Ghotbeddin Abul Muzaffar Ebadi, p. 129.
5. Ghotbeddin Abul Muzaffar Ebadi, p. 130.
6. Handwritten manuscript.
7. Attar Neyshapouri, *Tazkera-ol-Olia*, Teheran: 1942, p. 148.
8. Attar Neyshapouri, p. 149.

Chapter Eleven

1. Moulana Hussein Vaez Kashani Sabzevari, *Futovat Nameh Sultani*, Teheran: 1350 (1971), p. 52.
2. Moulana Hussein Vaez Kashani Sabzevari, p. 56.
3. Moulana Hussein Vaez Kashani Sabzevari, p. 55.
4. Moulana Hussein Vaez Kashani Sabzevari, pp. 52-55.
5. Abul Ghasem Ghosheiri, *Resaleh Ghosheiri*, p. 453.
6. Abul Ghasem Ghosheiri, p. 453.
7. Abul Ghasem Ghosheiri, p. 459.
8. Abul Ghasem Ghosheiri, pp. 461-463.
9. Abul Ghasem Ghosheiri, p. 464.
10. Ezeddin Mohammad Kashani, pp. 377-378.
11. Moulana Shah Maghsoud, *Serajol-Huda*, Teheran: 1357, p. 13.
12. Moulana Shah Maghsoud, p. 12.

Chapter Twelve

1. Ghotbeddin Abul Muzaffar Ebadi, p. 147.
2. Ghotbeddin Abul Muzaffar Ebadi, p. 206.

Further Reading and Bibliography

References and Suggested Readings: Non-English
Many of these books are written by ancient Sufis and philosophers edited and compiled by researchers and printed in the specified places and dates.

Abu Hamed Mohammad Ghazali, *Ehyael Oulum*, trans. from Arabic into Farsi, Mohammad Kharazmi,Teheran.
Abu Jafar Kuleini Razi, *Osul Kafi*, ed. Mohammad Akhundi, Teheran: 1334 (Solar/ equivalent to 1955).
Amir al Moumenin Ali, *Nahjul Balagheh*, compiled by Mohammad Ali Ansari, Teheran: 1345.
Abil Hassan Hajwiri, *Kashfol Mahjub*, Teheran: 1336.
Ali Kianfar, Ph. D. *Oveyse Gharan and His School*, California: 1983.
Abul Hassan Zarkub, Ph. D. *Arzesh-e-Miras-e-Sufieh*, Teheran: 1342.
Ezeddin Nassafi, *Insan-e- Ka'amel*, Teheran: 1341.
Ezeddin Mohammad Kashani, *Mesbahul Hedaye va Meftahol Kefaeh*, Teheran: 1325.
Einol Ghozat, *Mosanafat*, Teheran: 1341.
Einol Ghozat, *Tamhidat*, Teheran: 1341.
Einol Ghozat, *Zubdatol-Haghayegh*, Teheran: 1341.
Einol Ghozat, *Resaleh Yazdan Shenakht*, Teheran:1327.
Ezzeddin Abu Hamed, *Sharh-e-Nahjul Balagheh*, Beirut: 1374 (HL).
Fariddeddin Attar Neyshapouri, *Elahi Nameh*, Teheran.
Fariddeddin Attar Neyshapouri, *Mantagh al Teyr*, Teheran: 1341.
Fakhruddin Ibrahim Araghi, *Kuliat*, edited by Saiied Vaffisi, Teheran: 1338.
Ghosheiri, *Resaleh Ghosheiri*, edited and translated by Badiezaman Furozanfar, Teheran: 1346.
Ghotbeddin Abul Muzaffar Ebadi, *Sufi Nameh*, Teheran: 1347.
Ghazi Abu Bakr Balkhi, *Maghamat-e-Hamidi*, Tabriz: 1311.
Ghasem Ghani, Ph. D. *Bahsi dar Tasavuf*, Teheran: 1340.
Hafez Shiraz, *Divan*, Teheran.

Hazrat Mir Ghotbeddin Mohammad Angha, *Ershad Nameh*, handwritten.
Ibn Karbelai, *Ruzatol Jenan*, Teheran: 1344.
Imam Ahmad Ghazali, *Savaneh ol Oushagh*, Teheran.
Moulana Hussein Vaez Kashefi Sabzevari, *Futuvat Nameh*, Teheran: 1350.
Moulana Shah Maghsoud, *Nirvan*, Tehran: 1954.
Moulana Shah Maghsoud, *Payam-e-Del*, Tehran: 1954.
Moulana Shah Maghsoud, *Avazeh Khodayan*, Tehran: 1954.
Moulana Shah Maghsoud, *Magha'a a sedol ershad*, Tehran: 1978.
Moulana Shah Maghsoud, *Serajol Huda*, Tehran: 1978.
Mohammad Hussein Burhan, *Burhan-e-Ghatea*, Teheran: 1342.
Nahjul Fesahe, Saying narrated from Prophet Mohammad, trans. Abu Ghasem Payandeh, Teheran: 1345.
Rumi, *Masnavi-e-Maanavi*, Teheran.
Reza Gholi Hedayat, *Riyazol Aurefin*, Teheran: 1337.
Sheikh Najmeddin Razi, *Resaleh Eshgh va Aghl*, Teheran: 1345.
Sheikh Ahmad Ja'am, *Ruzatol Mazanabein va Janatol Mushtaghin*, Teheran: 1355.
Sheikh Ahmad Ja'am, *Onso Tabein va Seratolah Mubin*, Teheran: 1350.
Sheilh Najmeddin Razi, *Mersadol Eba'ad*, Teheran: 1352.
Sheikh Mahmud Shabestari, *Resaleh Haghol Yaghin*, Teheran: 1339.
Sheilh Ruzbehan Baghli, *Abharol Ausheghin*, Teheran: 1328.
Sheikh Abu Saiid Abul Khayr, *Asrare Tuhud*, Teheran.
Sheikh Ahmad Ja'am, *Hadighatol Haghigheh*, Teheran: 1343.
Sheikh Shahabeddin Suhrevardi, *Awarefol Mauref*, Cairo: 1318.
Sheikh Abu Ibrahim Sulami, *Arbain fi Tasavuf*, Heydar Abad: 1369.